Antique Stained Glass

for the home

Molly Higgins

Schiffer Publishing Ltd®

4880 Lower Valley Road, Atglen, PA 19310 USA

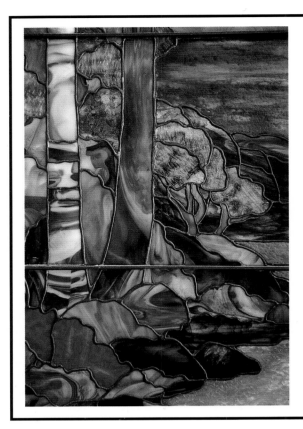

Dedication

This book is lovingly dedicated to my wonderful, wonderful family—my parents John and Lee and sister Susannah.

Title Page: Zipper-cut Fleur-de-lis design

Revised 2nd Edition
Copyright © 2005 by Schiffer Publishing
Library of Congress Control Number: 2004114907

Designed by John P. Cheek
Type set in Freeform 721 BT/Souvenir Lt BT

ISBN: 0-7643-2182-X
Printed in China
1 2 3 4

Published by Schiffer Publishing Ltd.
4880 Lower Valley Road
Atglen, PA 19310
Phone: (610) 593-1777; Fax: (610) 593-2002
E-mail: Info@schifferbooks.com

For the largest selection of fine reference books on this and related subjects, please visit our web site at
www.schifferbooks.com
We are always looking for people to write books on new and related subjects. If you have an idea for a book please contact us at the above address.

This book may be purchased from the publisher.
Include $3.95 for shipping.
Please try your bookstore first.
You may write for a free catalog.

In Europe, Schiffer books are distributed by
Bushwood Books
6 Marksbury Ave.
Kew Gardens
Surrey TW9 4JF England
Phone: 44 (0) 20 8392-8585; Fax: 44 (0) 20 8392-9876
E-mail: info@bushwoodbooks.co.uk
Free postage in the U.K., Europe; air mail at cost.

Contents

Acknowledgments 4

Introduction 5

Classic Influences in Decorative Windows 6
 Victorian 7
 John Lafarge and Louis Comfort Tiffany 8
 The Arts & Crafts Movement 10
  The Glasgow School 10
 Frank Lloyd Wright and the Prairie School 11
 Simpler Designs 12

Elements of Decorative Windows 13
 Glass 13
 Jewels 16
 Leading 16
 What is Authentic? 17

Chapter One: Sidelights, Transoms, & Other Rectangular Designs 18
 Abstract Designs 18
 Floral Designs 55
 Shields, Wreaths, & Fleurs-de-Lis 79

Chapter Two: Arches & Round Windows 99

Chapter Three: Designs in Clear Glass 118

Chapter Four: Painted & Etched Windows 140

Chapter Five: A Touch of Glass: Gallery of Manchester Windows 156

Bibliography 178

Appendix: Catalog Images 179

Acknowledgments

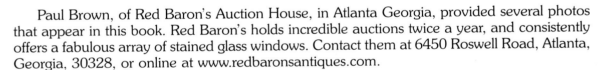

Bill Hylen, of Coming Up Roses Antiques in Adamstown, Pennsylvania, contributed time and insight to this project that I could not have done without. Not only did he allow us to shoot dozens and dozens of his windows, but he accompanied me on photo shoots, provided additional materials, and helped with research. Contact Bill at (610) 647-9543.

Richard Kurtz also provided many windows in this book. He has a fantastic assortment in his shop, many of which he has repaired or restored. Contact him at the Stained Glass Art Shop, 2503 Route 57, Stewartsville, New Jersey 08886, (908) 213-0242.

Paul Brown, of Red Baron's Auction House, in Atlanta Georgia, provided several photos that appear in this book. Red Baron's holds incredible auctions twice a year, and consistently offers a fabulous array of stained glass windows. Contact them at 6450 Roswell Road, Atlanta, Georgia, 30328, or online at www.redbaronsantiques.com.

Joel Zettler of Oley Valley Architectural Antiques, Ltd., in Denver, Pennsylvania, made his extensive stock of windows available to us and told us the local characteristics.

Dean Grimshaw, of the Hobbit Antiques, in Naches, Washington, has collected unusual stained glass windows for many years. He kindly offered to have us photograph some of them and encouraged us in this project.

Stuart Grannen, President, and Patrick Ottesen, of Architectural Artifacts, Inc., in Chicago, Illinois, shared their large knowledge and inventory of windows and put us in touch with private collectors who were most enthusiastic about this book.

Helene Weiss, of Willet Stained Glass Studios in Philadelphia, Pennsylvania, spent time with us in the early stages of this project and provided us with insight and direction. Her love for and knowledge of stained glass is tremendous, and we are so grateful for her willingness to share her expertise.

Bruce Waters did outstanding work with photography for this book. Doug Congdon-Martin and Blair Loughrey also made welcome contributions of their skill and knowledge of photography. Nancy Schiffer put invaluable effort into to this project; none of this would have been possible without her.

A warm thank-you goes to the Etzweiler family not only for allowing me to shoot their windows, but for many years of friendship and hospitality.

Finally, I must thank my three boys, Michael, Jesse, and Michael for showing me that rainy days make the sunny ones so much better. I love you guys!

Introduction

Nothing can transform a room quite like a decorative window. Its appearance can vary widely; different types of light can bring out a full spectrum of hues and textures in the glass. In the morning, it might have a gentle, muted glow. In the late afternoon, it might sparkle brilliantly as the sun sinks lower in the sky.

In the years surrounding 1900, American and European architects and interior designers often used ornamental glass windows to enhance homes and other buildings. They were produced in all shapes and sizes, inspired by a variety of creative visions of their time, and included wonderful array of gorgeous glasses and techniques. These windows regularly appear on today's antiques market, many at reasonable prices. People are discovering the timeless elegance of these windows, and they are joining a rapidly growing field of collecting.

Decorative windows have a distinct element of mystery in that it is quite difficult to link them to the artisans who created them. Rarely are these windows signed, and it is a complicated undertaking to pick out stylistic subtleties that would classify the work of a single artist or company. However, each individual window is a fascinating study unto itself, with its own combination of glass and workmanship.

This guide is designed to introduce you to the wide world of antique decorative windows. It is a gallery through which you can stroll, with an array of windows ranging from the very complex to the very simple. It is not an historical survey, nor does it include ground-breaking research. There are thousands of unanswered questions surrounding these windows, but the one we will focus on here is "which will look best in *your* house?"

Classic Influences in Decorative Windows

In the late nineteenth century, several styles of architecture and interior design evolved in America and Europe. At the same time, the production of decorative windows was at its peak of quality. They played a role in the creative visions of many styles, adding new dimensions in color and light.

In many cases it is difficult to classify a window, as they were often composed using elements of more than one style. Here we will briefly touch on some of the influences on stained glass around the turn of the twentieth century.

Victorian

The Victorian age saw tremendous development in both Europe and America, and a wealth of money and materials allowed for marvelous expressions of style. In his book *Great Glass in American Architecture,* H. Weber Wilson warns of the inaccuracy of referring to American decorative windows as "Victorian," as the Victorian style was much more of a British phenomenon. However, during the last quarter of the nineteenth century, many windows were produced in America with a complexity and care for detail characteristic of Victorian style. As a result these windows are often described as "Victorian." These windows have ornate designs, grand flourishes, and they frequently glitter with jewels. They often combine elements of the Neo-Gothic style also popular in Great Britain at the time.

Victorian window with crescent moon and owl design. Ripple and opalescent glass, jewels. 35" x 77". *Courtesy Paul Brown, Red Baron's Antiques.* $2995

1890s Victorian window with ripple and other textured glass. 22" square. *Courtesy Coming Up Roses Antiques.* $850

American three-panel window by John La Farge, c. 1880, in original iron frame, probably lower half of the full original window. 58 5/8"w. *Courtesy Architectural Artifacts, Inc. Chicago.*

Later Tiffany church window, c. 1925.

Detail.

In the realm of stained glass, the names Tiffany and La Farge are perhaps the most readily recognized. Both men created stunning masterpieces in stained glass, but their contributions to the craft reach further. John La Farge, a talented painter, is credited with developing the use of opalescent glass in leaded windows. While decorating Trinity Church in Boston, Massachusetts, La Farge wanted to create windows that allowed more light to pass through than the traditional stained glass windows of the time. He found a solution in his soap dish, made of a newly developed translucent glass made to resemble porcelain. La Farge worked with the Heidt glassworks to develop sheets of this glass in different colors, and used them in his windows with a layering technique to achieve marvelous effects. La Farge pooled his efforts with Louis Comfort Tiffany, who was at Heidt glassworks at the time, to explore this new direction in glass. However, the friendship ended quickly; Tiffany procured the patent rights to opalescent glass in a long court battle with La Farge.

Tiffany established his own glassworks to produce the type of glass needed to execute his designs. Plated in layers of rich opalescent glass, Tiffany's windows are magnificent, manipulating color, shading, and light to create breathtaking scenes. Of course, Tiffany's work in leaded glass was not limited to windows—he also worked in three dimensions to create lamps and other objects.

It is interesting that windows by even the most prominent name in stained glass are difficult to identify. Tiffany's design company grew to employ hundreds of artisans, who worked on a freelance basis and often simultaneously for other companies. In addition, only a relatively small number of Tiffany's works have been signed. As a result, proving the authenticity of a Tiffany window is often a hot debate.

The craftsmanship of leaded windows lends itself to the Arts & Crafts Movement of Europe and America in the late nineteenth and early twentieth centuries. The Movement originated with William Morris in England, whose design company is credited with many gorgeous windows. In an age where machines and technology were gaining momentum, Morris saw the importance of handcrafted items in interior design. Arts & Crafts communities were established that produced a full spectrum of decorations for the home, from furniture, to metalwork, to ceramics, to textiles, to decorative windows.

The Arts & Crafts influence appears in decorative windows through linear, stylized designs in colorful opalescent glass. These windows have an understated elegance, and can include landscapes, fruit, and flowers.

The Glasgow School

One brand of Arts ad Crafts influence that appears in decorative windows originates in Glasgow, Scotland. Charles Rennie Mackintosh was an architect who also had distinct concepts of interior design. Mackintosh, Herbert MacNair, and Margaret and Frances Macdonald were known as the "Glasgow Four," and collaborated on unique decorative schemes. Mackintosh preferred muted solid colors in his designs, using leaded glass and ornate metalwork in place of prints and patterns. His window designs have a distinct style, combining stylized elements of Arts & Crafts with both curves and sharp angles.

Sidelight with colorful Arts & Crafts design. 9 1/4" x 55". *Courtesy Oley Valley Architectural Antiques.* $550

Glasgow School design. 27 1/4" x 26 3/4". *Courtesy Architectural Artifacts, Inc. Chicago.* $465

Frank Lloyd Wright and the Prairie School

In the late nineteenth century, the wide-open expanse of the Midwestern United States landscape fostered a unique ideal of architecture and design known as the Prairie School. Architects and artisans working in this style merged the functionality of materials with an imaginative, natural optimism, sentiments characteristic of the middle class toward which their designs were geared. At the forefront of this movement was Frank Lloyd Wright, a Chicago architect whose work, among others, marks the dawn of a modern age of design in America. Wright's open, airy structures were excellent environments for decorative windows. Recognizing this, he included them liberally, creating fascinating designs that were executed by local stained glass studios. His windows emphasized the vertical, and the use of much stiffer zinc caming eliminated the need for horizontal cross bars that would show through and conflict with the design.

Prairie School windows often combine tight, intricate geometric designs with open areas that do not interfere with the view outside or into the adjacent room. These windows are very linear, but also incorporate natural elements like trees, flowers, and leaves.

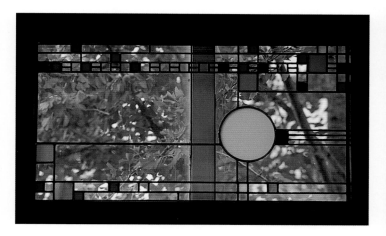

Window designed by Frank Lloyd Wright for the Avery-Coonley Playhouse, Riverside, Illinois, 1912. 33" x 17".

Frank Lloyd Wright, "Tree of Life" design. Designed for Darwin-Martin House, Buffalo, New York, 1904. 25 1/4" x 40 1/2". *Collection of Seymour Persky.* $1795

Simple arched design in cathedral and opalescent glass. 29" x 19". *Courtesy Coming Up Roses Antiques.* $300

The late nineteenth century was a high point in the production of decorative windows in America. However, in the years following the turn of the century, interest in decorative windows for the home dwindled as architectural tastes changed. Once-busy stained glass studios competed for business with increasing ferocity. Foreign competition and rising costs of labor and materials also helped to push the American stained glass industry towards a bleak future. Members of the industry attempted to alter the course by forming the National Ornamental Glass Manufacturer's Association in 1903. Among the efforts made by the association was the 1909 creation of an "Official Catalogue" of stained glass designs to be used by studios nationwide. This catalogue was loaded with simple, standardized windows that were fixed in both cost and design, in hopes of eliminating competition between studios. Windows that may have been inspired by this catalog appear in today's antiques marketplace; they are simple and bland, with few embellishments like jewels or fancy glass.

Elements of Decorative Windows

Glass

Glass is oviously the most significant part of a decorative window, and it has been produced in an incredible variety. This section is intended to acquaint you with a few of the different types of glass you will encounter when looking at windows.

Cathedral Glass

This is the most common variety of glass found in leaded windows. Usually machine made with a rolled technique, it is uniform in color and thickness. Often you will see small air bubbles lodged in it. Cathedral glass can be seen in a variety of colors and textures.

Fluted Glass

A type of glass associated with Philadelphia and the surrounding Pennsylvania area. Often known as refrigerator glass, it has evenly spaced flutes running parallel to one another. The texture lends itself nicely to decorative windows.

Opalescent Glass

Another commonly found variety of glass, opalescent glass has been made in a variety of textures and infinite combinations of colors. The development of this glass for use in windows is attributed to John La Farge; Louis Comfort Tiffany's studio later produced an outstanding array of opalescent glass. Opalescent glass can be hard to match when restoring older windows, as the types produced at the turn of the century differ greatly from those produced today. One of the interesting attributes of opalescent glass is that it is colorful even when there is no light shining through it, which can make a window look good both at night and from outside.

Opalescent Glass

Ripple Glass

A textured glass that frequently appears in decorative windows, frequently on opalescent glass. The ripple texture is rolled on while the glass is still molten, and can be either fine (known as spaghetti ripple) or wide.

Textured Glass

There is a large number of various textures of glass that are made with rollers while a sheet of glass is still hot. Many of these textures have descriptive names, including hammered glass, ripple glass, alligator glass, granite glass, and dozens of others.

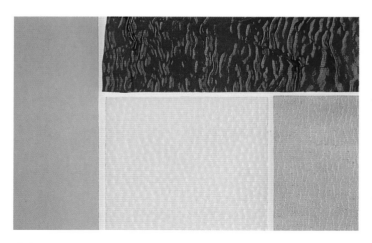

Colored textured glass, including ripple (red), hammered (light yellow).

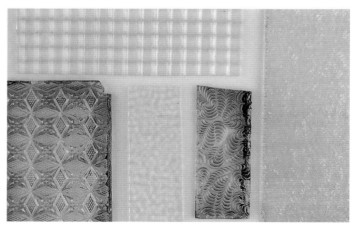

Clear textured glass.

Flashed Glass

Flashed glass is a clear pane of glass with a very thin layer of color is "flashed" onto the surface. The surface can then be etched to reveal the clear glass under the surface. Red is the most commonly found color.

Crackle Glass

Crackle glass is created by dipping a molten cylinder of glass in water, which "crackles" the outside of the glass while the inner layer stays warm. The cylinder is then sliced down the side and flattened to form a sheet.

Glue-chip Glass

A pane of glass is covered with a layer of animal glue and then heated in a drying oven; the glue contracts, leaving a crackled, feathery texture.

Glue-chip glass.

Beveled Glass

Beveled glass has edges that are tapered at an angle. In decorative windows, beveled glass is nearly always clear.

Window made of beveled glass highlighted by zipper cuts.

Drapery Glass

Drapery glass is a sign of quality in antique windows. It has varying thickness with irregular ripples that are created when the glass maker pushes a hot sheet of glass across a tabletop into folds resembling fabric drapery. The development of this technique is attributed to Louis Comfort Tiffany.

Acid-Etching

The creation of an image on a pane of glass (often flashed glass) by first covering it with a layer of acid-resistant paraffin or similar substance, scratching out the design, and then disintegrating the exposed areas using hydroflouric acid. An alternative to this dangerous procedure involves stencils and sandblasting.

Manganese

Manganese Oxide is used to tint clear glass a violet shade. Clear glass in antique windows also has amounts of manganese, which will tint the clear glass a violet shade as the sun shines through it over a period of many years.

Vaseline Glass

A type of glass very similar in color to petroleum jelly, hence its name. It carries slightly radioactive properties detectable with a Geiger Counter. It glows a neon green under a black light.

Vaseline jewels with clear crackle glass on each side and textured glass above.

Jewels

Jewels are a wonderful addition to decorative windows. They appear in many sizes, shapes, and textures, adding color, dimension, and texture to a window. They were used most widely before the turn of the century. As window designs became simpler, jewels were used less and less.

Roundels

Roundels are round spun discs, larger than jewels, that have a mark in the center from where the glass was separated from the punty.

A colorful assortment of jewels, including pinch-back, faceted, and pressed.

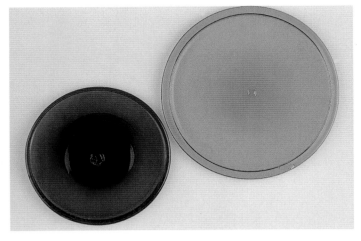

Roundels.

Leading

Decorative windows are held together by I-shaped strips of lead or similar material, known as caming. Usually cames are made of lead, although zinc and copper are also used. Zinc caming became popular after the turn of the century, and is much stiffer and difficult to work with when repairing antique windows.

Lead is by far the most common type of caming in decorative windows. The condition of the leading should play a significant role in your assessment of a window in the marketplace. Old lead means you will probably need to have the window releaded. New lead means that it probably already was, and that you should take a good look at the glass for replaced panels and embellishments.

Sometimes you will find windows in the marketplace that are warped and buckled. A short-term solution for this is to lay the window flat on a warm driveway or patio, so that the heat of the sun will even the window back out. However, lead begins to disintegrate after about a hundred years, so most original turn-of-the-century windows you find will certainly need to be releaded. When you are examining the window, look for pitting in the lead; this is a sign of old age.

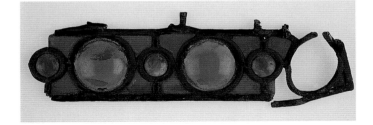

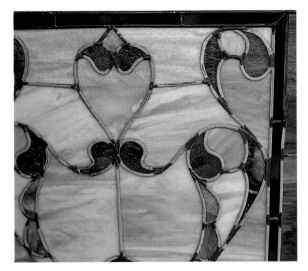

Pitted leading.

What is Authentic?

The life of a decorative window only begins with the artisans who produce it. The windows available on today's market have more stories to tell, however, as they have often been altered in various ways over the years. Glass panes are easily broken, and leading deteriorates over time. It is difficult to remove a leaded window from its installation in an old structure, and many windows are damaged by people trying to salvage them from buildings marked for destruction.

There are many shades of gray between an "original" antique window and a restored one. Some collectors, of course, value an original window—no matter how many panes have cracked or how badly the leading has warped—over one that has been liberally repaired with newer glass and leading. It is difficult, however, to determine that a window is fully unadulterated, because there is often no way to determine what it first looked like.

The restoration process is unique to each window and the artist at work on it. It can be a real challenge to match the older glass pieces with new glass. Some windows are in such disrepair that only parts of them can be salvaged; the central design of a large window might be extracted and set in a smaller frame, or a pair of matching windows with missing pieces might be merged into one complete window. Some restoration artists choose to add embellishments, like more jewels or an extra border. A variety of windows appears in this book, from the relatively untouched to the heavily embellished.

Keep this information in mind when you are pricing windows in the marketplace; a window is only worth what you are willing to pay for it. Make sure you examine the window closely. Are there panes of glass that don't quite match the color or texture of surrounding panes, suggesting they were replaced? Does the leading shine, or does it have a dark patina? Is the frame original, or is it new? These are all questions to ask when you are assessing decorative windows. Whatever type of window you are looking for, make sure you know what you are buying.

Chapter One
Sidelights, Transoms, and Other Rectangular Designs

Abstract Designs

Purple trefoil with jewels. 41" x 12". *Courtesy Oley Valley Architectural Antiques.* $1495

Two smaller windows from a residence in Baltimore, c. 1897. Ripple and opalescent glass, jewels. Left, 6" x 41½". Right, 6" x 21". *Courtesy of Bill Hylen.* $400 each.

Transom window with colorful leaf forms on an oxblood opalescent background. 34¾" x 15¾". *Courtesy Oley Valley Architectural Antiques.* $995

Transom window with detailed design, on a background of different textured clear glass, bordered in jewels. *Courtesy of Bill Hylen.* $750

Textured glass with four pink jewels. 24" x 23". *Courtesy Oley Valley Architectural Antiques.* $495.

Victorian window with crescent moon and owl design. Ripple and opalescent glass, jewels. 35" x 77". *Courtesy Paul Brown, Red Baron's Antiques.* $2995

Red, purple, and pink glass with scrolled design. 36¼" x 26¼". *Courtesy Architectural Artifacts, Inc. Chicago.* $795

Opalescent and ripple glass. 27½" x 7", c. 1880. $450

Opalescent glass with jewels. 26½" x 14½". *Courtesy Oley Valley Architectural Antiques.* $450

Opalescent and beveled glass with intricate leadwork. *Courtesy of Bill Hylen.* $800

Scrolls with jewels, pink border. 43½" x 11½". *Courtesy Oley Valley Architectural Antiques.* $650

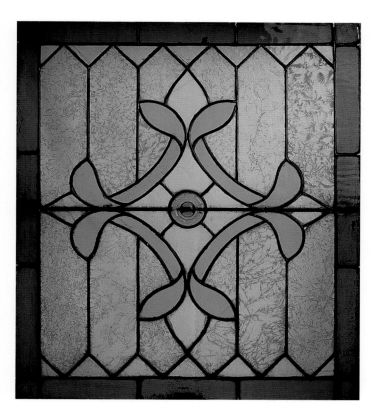

Glue chip glass, pressed jewel in center. *Courtesy of Bill Hylen.* $350

Striking blue border. This window is slightly bowed with aged leading. 13¾" x 25". *Courtesy Oley Valley Architectural Antiques.* $395

23

Window from a Pittsburgh, Pennsylvania residence. Intricate design with rich opalescent hues. 52" x 58".
Courtesy Paul Brown, Red Baron's Antiques. $2795

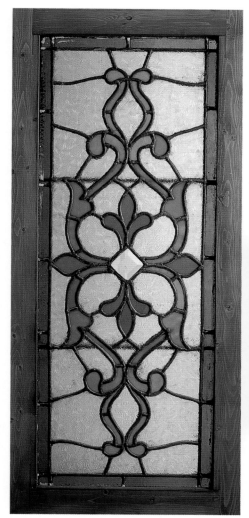

Door panel with beveled jewel in center and unique textured glass. Set of two. 17½" x 39½". *Courtesy of Bill Hylen.* $400 for one, $800 for the set of two.

Fan design. 29½" x 10½". *Courtesy Oley Valley Architectural Antiques.* $495

Vibrant window with pressed jewels and red oxblood opalescent glass. 39" x 9¾". *Courtesy Oley Valley Architectural Antiques.* $795

Victorian-style design with unique opalescent glass in center. Note how the yellow opalescent glass in the central design has been cut so that the swirls in the glass complement the design. c. 1925. 23½" x 37". *Courtesy of Richard Kurtz.* $995

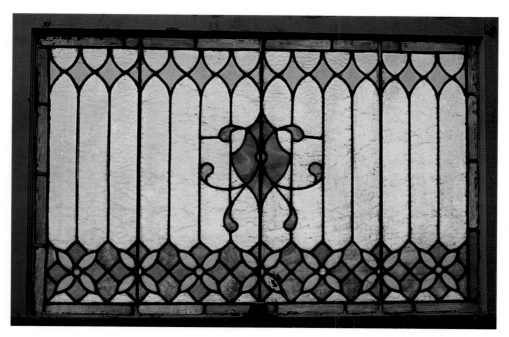

Intricate design with hammmered and opalescent glass. 23" x 36". *Courtesy of Bill Hylen.* $500 alone or $1500 set of three.

Stained Glass Mosaics

Stained glass mosaics do not appear in the marketplace too often, although they are still out there. These fantastic windows are composed of thousands of small pieces of glass (often in triangular cuts) arranged in complex designs in rich colors. They more closely resemble a mosaic than a leaded window; the substance between the the pieces of glass looks more like a dark grout than caming, and was evidently poured in a molten state. These intricate windows are credited to Henry Belcher Studios, which briefly produced them in the late 1800s. There has been speculation that Belcher's unique "leading" process involved the use of mercury, which posed a serious health hazard to the artisans at work and explains why the windows were only produced for a short time.

Mosaic pair with small jewels. 1880s-90s. 14" x 16". Slightly buckled. *Courtesy of Bill Hylen.* $2500/pair.

Window from a residence in Pasaic, New Jersey. c. 1890s. Opalescent and ripple glass. 19½" x 40½". *Courtesy of Richard Kurtz.* $1000

Ornate design with faceted jewels. 21¼" x 19½". *Courtesy Oley Valley Architectural Antiques.* $650

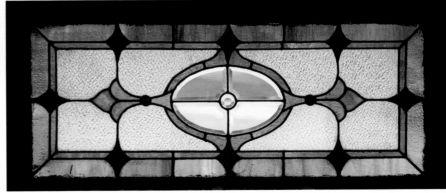

Window from the coal region of Pennsylvania. Beveled glass center. 39" x 15½". $695

Door with red border, fluted glass, and clear jewels. 13" x 48½". *Courtesy Oley Valley Architectural Antiques.* $3795 pr.

Fine leadwork with opalescent glass. Drapery glass—a sign of quality in earlier windows—was used for the shells to simulate the scallop texture. *Courtesy of Bill Hylen.* $995

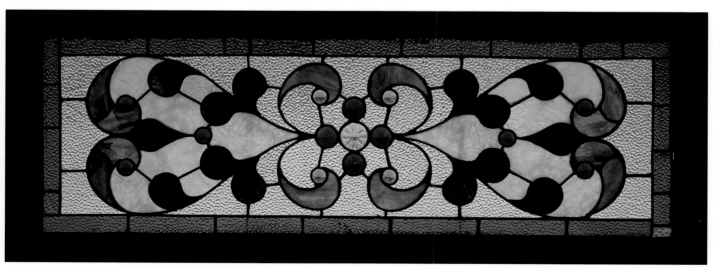

Opalescent and textured glass with jewels and orange border. 43½" x 13¾". *Courtesy Oley Valley Architectural Antiques.* $1150

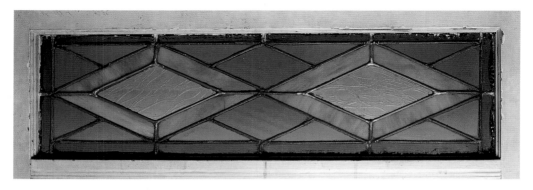

Diamond design with crackle, opalescent, and cathedral glass. Note the difference in leading between the central and background areas. *Courtesy of Bill Hylen.* $195

Sunbeam design with ribbon. It appears this window is the top half of a double-hung window. 21½" x 28". *Courtesy Oley Valley Architectural Antiques.* $675

Transom window with different textures and opalescent glass. *Courtesy of Bill Hylen.* $295

Matching pair of windows, opalescent and cathedral glass. Each measures 12" x 12". *Courtesy of Bill Hylen.* $95 each.

Rectangular window with three jewels. Note how the opalescent glass has been cut to complement the design. 11½" x 30". *Courtesy Oley Valley Architectural Antiques.* $450

Ripple and opalescent glass. 43½" x 13¾". *Courtesy Oley Valley Architectural Antiques.* $895

This window allegedly was first installed in a brothel in Houston, Texas. It is a combination window, with both colored and clear glass, and large jewels. 57" x 18". c. 1890s. *Courtesy of Richard Kurtz.* $3500

Combination Windows

These unique designs feature both clear beveled and colored glass. They are commonly called "combination" windows and are associated with the midwestern United States.

Walnut door. Beveled and stained glass with jewels, arched top. 11¾" x 40". *Courtesy Oley Valley Architectural Antiques.* $3495 pr.

Contemporary window with beveled and stained glass. 39¾" x 60". *Courtesy Architectural Artifacts, Inc. Chicago.* $2495

Combination window, scrolled and beveled center, clear and textured colored glasses. Note how the central yellow panes smoothly blend from a dark shade at the bottom to a much lighter shade at the top. 32¾" x 52". *Courtesy Hobbit Antiques.* $3595

Chicago combination window. Spaghetti, ripple glass. 40" x 19½". *Courtesy of Richard Kurtz.* $2700.

Chicago combination window, 1890. 14" x 40". *Courtesy of Richard Kurtz.* $2800.

Gorgeous window in need of repair. Many intricate cuts, many small and large chunk jewels (note border), many different types of glass. Note the drapery glass on the white flowers. 46½" x 16". c. 1890s. *Courtesy of Richard Kurtz.* $8000 as is.

American Victorian window with pressed jewels and beveled center. 23½" x 47". *Courtesy Architectural Artifacts, Inc. Chicago.* $1695

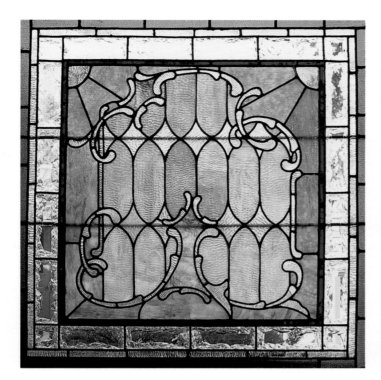

Assymetrical design in rippled opalescent glasses. Interesting chipped bevel border. 34" square. *Courtesy Hobbit Antiques.* $695

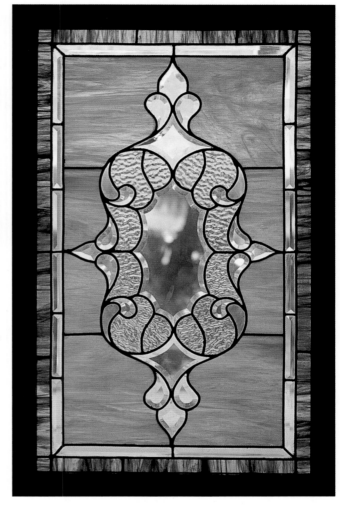

Window from Buffalo, New York. The outer border is new, and the inner design includes ripple and beveled clear glass, surrounded by blue opalescent. The lead is pitted and the clear glass has the purple sun-tint from manganese. c. 1900 18" x 30". *Courtesy of Richard Kurtz.* $900

Victorian design with alligator glass (border, white flower), ripple glass, and jewels. *Courtesy of Bill Hylen.* $600.

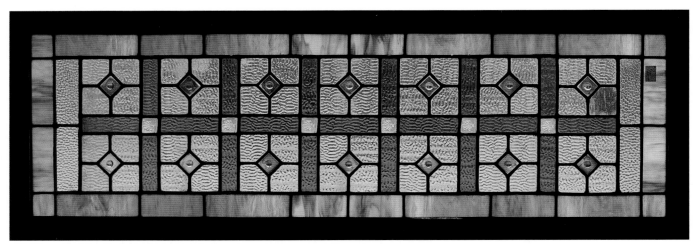

Woven design with pink opalescent border and square jewels. c. 1880. 58¾" x 17". *Courtesy Oley Valley Architectural Antiques.* $895

American Victorian fan design with jewels. 17¾" square. *Courtesy Architectural Artifacts, Inc. Chicago.* $950/pr.

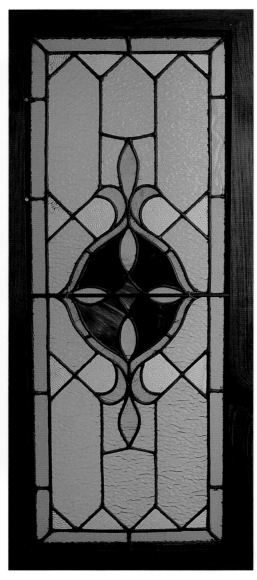

Dark opalescent in center design, surrounded by textured glass. *Courtesy of Bill Hylen.* $295

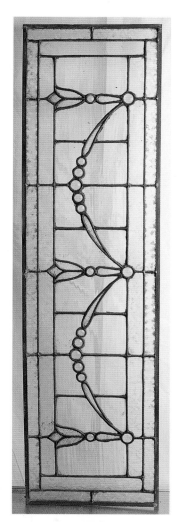

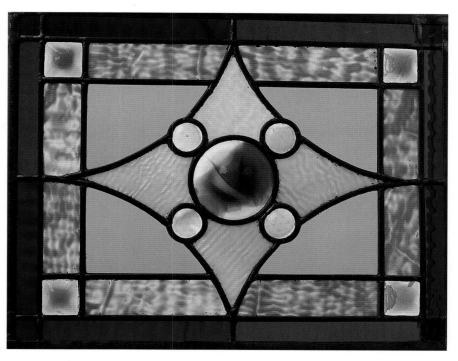

Marbled roundel and jewels with ripple, opalescent, and red flashed ripple glass. 13" x 16½". *Courtesy of Bill Hylen.* $450.

Clear design with textured, fluted, glue chip, and ripple glass. The jewels are made of vaseline glass. 44½" x 12". *Courtesy of Bill Hylen.* $500

Window from Newark, New Jersey, c. 1920s. Opalescent glass, pitted lead. 18½" x 22". *Courtesy of Richard Kurtz.* $395

Crackle glass with roundel in center. *Courtesy of Bill Hylen.* $295.

Later window with earlier Victorian influence. Opalescent glass. c. 1925. *Courtesy of Richard Kurtz.* $725

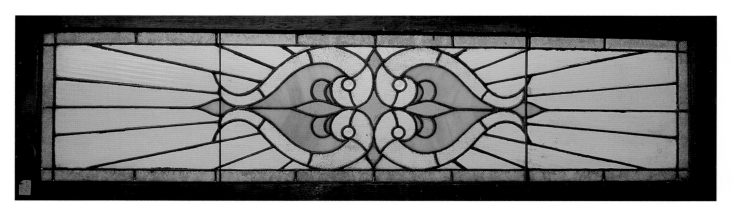

Fluted, hammered, and textured glass, with four jewels in the center. *Courtesy of Bill Hylen.* $695

Opalescent glass design with two jewels and beveled glass in center. 31" x 10". *Courtesy Oley Valley Architectural Antiques.* $495

Victorian-style window that appears to have been repaired more than once in its lifetime. Intricate design in different textures of glass with clusters of jewels. 33" x 33". *Courtesy of Bill Hylen.* $795

Gorgeous window with geometric pattern in the center, surrounded by a red and blue scroll design. Intricate leading and cuts of glass. 21¼" x 62½". *Courtesy Hobbit Antiques.* $1595

Numbered transom, green and yellow. 31½" x 11½". *Courtesy Architectural Artifacts, Inc. Chicago.* $150

19th century patchwork design, cathedral glass. *Courtesy of Bill Hylen.* $295

Patchwork transom that originally included a painted-on number. Made of cathedral glass, this window has had a lot of repair work done to it. 48" x 18". *Courtesy of Bill Hylen.* $500

Patchwork design in ripple glass with white flower in center and faceted jewels. 35½" x 11½". *Courtesy Oley Valley Architectural Antiques.* $595

Patchwork design with cross in center and pressed jewels with striations. 43½" x 14½". 1880s-90s. *Courtesy of Bill Hylen.* $495

Flowers with patchwork design, originally part of a door. *Courtesy of Bill Hylen.* $695.

Patchwork design with arched-top border. 10¾" x 19½". *Courtesy Oley Valley Architectural Antiques.* $395

Colorful window with beveled glass, jewels, and patchwork design in center. 32¼" x 12½". *Courtesy Oley Valley Architectural Antiques.* $595

Window from the coal region of Pennsylvania. Cut glass center. 36" x 15". $650

Rectangular window with blown roundels, white bull's eyes, and red flashed glass. 66" x 12". *Courtesy Oley Valley Architectural Antiques.* $1495

Arts & Crafts style window from Easton, Pennsylvania, c. 1925. 20" x 27½". *Courtesy of Richard Kurtz.* $600

Aesthetic Movement window. Opalescent glass, vaseline jewels. 24" x 65". *Courtesy Paul Brown, Red Baron's Antiques.* $2695

Right: Asymmetrical Aesthetic Movement window. Opalescent glass, jewels. 39" square. *Courtesy Paul Brown, Red Baron's Antiques.* $995

Arts & Crafts style design with textured glass. 34" x18". *Courtesy of Bill Hylen.* $150

All opalescent glass, no frame. Frameless windows usually require a new strip of lead around the edge so they don't fall apart. 12" x 32½". *Courtesy of Bill Hylen.* $195

Arts & Crafts design with four green trees. 21¼" x 51½". *Courtesy Architectural Artifacts, Inc. Chicago.* $695

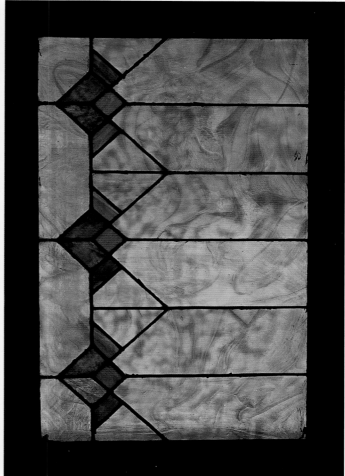

Arts & Crafts design made entirely of art glass, c. 1920s. 16" x 26". *Courtesy of Richard Kurtz.* $250

Sidelight with geometric Arts & Crafts design. 8" x 64". *Courtesy of Bill Hylen.* $450

Sidelight from Toledo, Ohio with ripple glass and jewels. 1890-1895. 10½" x 46". *Courtesy of Richard Kurtz.* $3295

Transom window, 51" x 17". *Courtesy Oley Valley Architectural Antiques.* $795

Right: Arts & Crafts style window with windmill design. Opalescent glass. 34" x 54". *Courtesy Paul Brown, Red Baron's Antiques.* $1495

Sidelight with colorful Arts & Crafts design. 9¼" x 55". *Courtesy Oley Valley Architectural Antiques.* $650

Arts & Crafts design. Top, 21¾" x 25½". Bottom, 21¾" x 37¼". *Courtesy Oley Valley Architectural Antiques.* $150 ea.

American Arts & Crafts window. 18" x 32". *Courtesy Architectural Artifacts, Inc. Chicago.* $975

Arts & Crafts design, house with sun. Note the many colors and types of glass, accented by an equally colorful border. 40" x 20". *Courtesy of Richard Kurtz.* $1795

Arts & Crafts design. 37¼" x 21½". *Courtesy Architectural Artifacts, Inc. Chicago.* $1200

Arts & Crafts design. 43¾" x 21¾". *Courtesy Architectural Artifacts, Inc. Chicago.* $1100

Prairie School

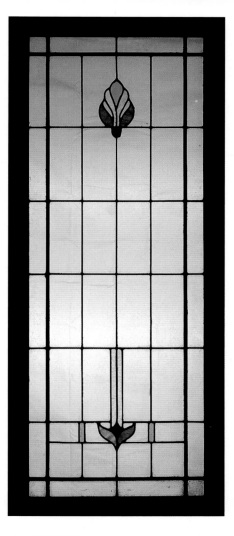

Prairie School design. 17¼" x 47". *Courtesy Architectural Artifacts, Inc. Chicago.* $365

Prairie School design. 17½" x 25½". *Courtesy Architectural Artifacts, Inc. Chicago.* $425

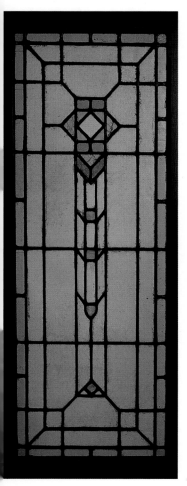

Prairie School influence. Geometric, beveled glass in center. *Courtesy of Bill Hylen.* $500.

Prairie School design. 25¼" x 27¾". *Courtesy Architectural Artifacts, Inc. Chicago.* $365

Two-part Prairie School design with white rectangle leaf center. Arched top, in copper frame. 23"w x 18-½"h. *Courtesy Architectural Artifacts, Inc. Chicago.* $895

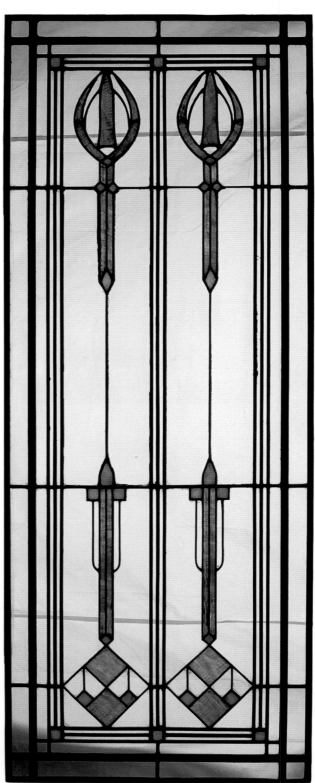

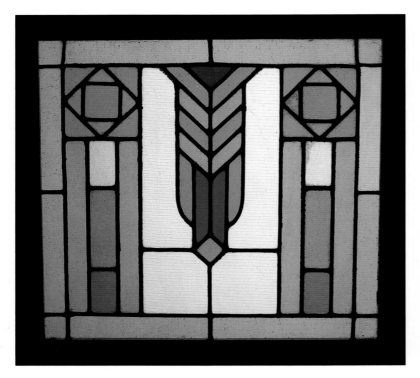

Prairie School influence, c. 1910-20. 19½" x 18". *Courtesy Oley Valley Architectural Antiques.* $295

Prairie School design. 23" x 62". *Courtesy Architectural Artifacts, Inc. Chicago.* $1595

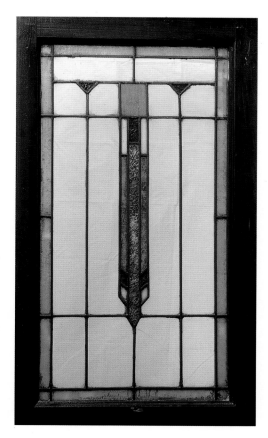

Prairie School design. 15" x 29". *Courtesy Architectural Artifacts, Inc. Chicago.* $225

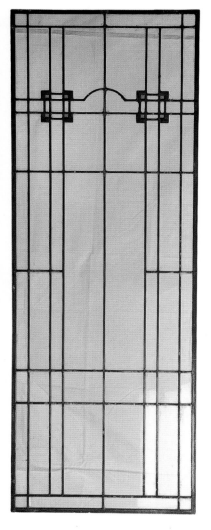

English design with copper caming. 15" x 43". *Courtesy Architectural Artifacts, Inc. Chicago.* $625

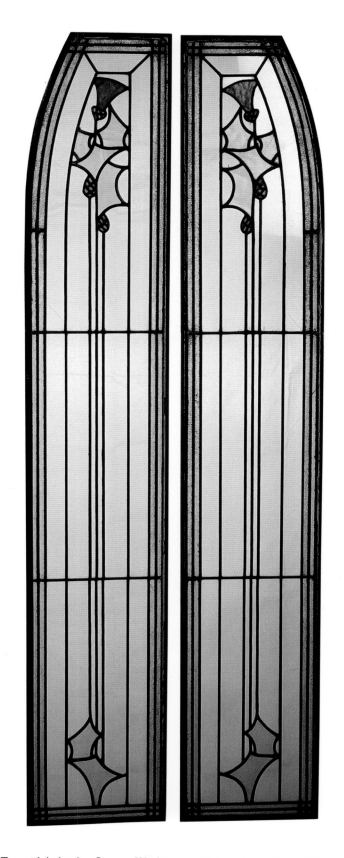

Two sidelights by George Washington Maher. A member of the Prairie School, he was known for his "motif-rhythm" theory of design that unified both the interior and exterior of a home with a common decorative motif, usually composed of a natural image and geometric shape. 9¼" x 60". *Courtesy Architectural Artifacts, Inc. Chicago.* $795 ea.

Prairie school design. 23" x 33"w. *Courtesy Architectural Artifacts, Inc. Chicago.* $795

Prairie school design by George Mann Niedecken. Neidecken was an architect who collaborated with Frank Lloyd Wright on several significant designs, such as the Robie, Coonley, and Dana houses. Later he ran an interior design firm that produced furniture and other items for Prairie School architects. Top glass, 48" x 27". Bottom glass, 48" x 75"h. *Courtesy Architectural Artifacts, Inc. Chicago.* $1795 set.

Glasgow, Scotland School design. 17½" x 30¾". *Courtesy Architectural Artifacts, Inc. Chicago.* $695

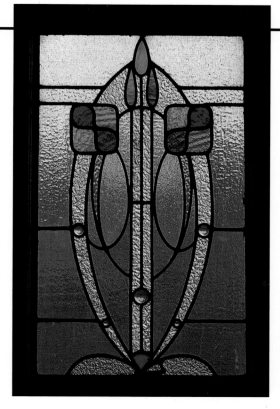

Glasgow School design. 16¾" x 28". *Courtesy Architectural Artifacts, Inc. Chicago.* $695

Glasgow School design. 27¼" x 26¾". *Courtesy Architectural Artifacts, Inc. Chicago.* $465

Glasgow School design. 36" x 28". *Courtesy Architectural Artifacts, Inc. Chicago.* $895

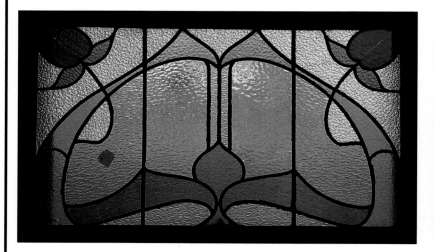

Glasgow School design. 36" x 20¼". *Courtesy Architectural Artifacts, Inc. Chicago.* $595

Glasgow School design. 16½" x 44¾". *Courtesy Architectural Artifacts, Inc. Chicago.* $765

Glasgow School design. 43½" x 46". *Courtesy Architectural Artifacts, Inc. Chicago.* $995

Floral Designs

Floral design in opalescent glass. 1910-20. 20" x 45½". *Courtesy of Bill Hylen.* $750

Beveled, stained, and jeweled landing window originally from a Cincinnati, Ohio residence. 40" x 60". *Courtesy Paul Brown, Red Baron's Antiques.*

Victorian design with jewels, pressed jewel in center. 20¾" x 10½". *Courtesy Architectural Artifacts, Inc. Chicago.* $265

Clear background with interesting leading. 32½" x 31¾". *Courtesy Architectural Artifacts, Inc. Chicago.* $1200

Right: Sidelight with large roundels at top and bottom. 1890s. *Courtesy of Richard Kurtz.* $2500/Pair

Left: 1890s Victorian window with ripple and other textured glass. 22" square. *Courtesy of Bill Hylen.* $850

Textured glass, many colors, fine leadwork. c. 1900. Each measures 18" x 33". *Courtesy of Bill Hylen.* $1500/pair.

Assymetrical plant design. Early 20th century. 15" x 33½". *Courtesy of Bill Hylen.* $400

Victorian floral design with pressed jewels. 11½" x 37¾". *Courtesy Architectural Artifacts, Inc. Chicago.* $950

Large elaborate window from a school in Toledo, Ohio. 48" x 180". *Courtesy Paul Brown, Red Baron's Antiques.* $5500

Two-part window, granite and opalescent glass, small jewels. Each measures 22" x 36". *Courtesy of Bill Hylen.* $1500/pair.

English arched window with lilies, c. 1840. *Courtesy Architectural Artifacts, Inc. Chicago.* $825

Simple leaf design with cathedral glass. 18" x 46". *Courtesy of Bill Hylen.* $295

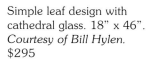

Window from Pasaic, New Jersey. Art glass, ripple glass, shaded chunk jewels. Pitted lead. 1890s. 26½" x 48". *Courtesy of Richard Kurtz.* $2695

Window from Washington, New Jersey. Note the darker opalescent glass. 15½" x 15". *Courtesy of Richard Kurtz.* $650

1890s window with English muffle glass and many jewels. 18" x 46". *Courtesy of Richard Kurtz.* $4600

Floral design in many colors and textures. 20" x 59". *Courtesy Architectural Artifacts, Inc. Chicago.* $1895

Flowers, jewels, ripple opalescent glass. Interesting blue and white flower. 1890s. 40" x 18". *Courtesy of Bill Hylen.* $600 as is, $1000 restored.

Close-up of blue and white opalescent glass.

Floral design with jewels. 47½" x 25". *Courtesy Oley Valley Architectural Antiques.* $1195

Intricate floral design with sunrise, perfectly symmetrical. 34" square. *Courtesy Paul Brown, Red Baron's Antiques.* $1895

American Victorian landing window with lots of jewels. Note how the glass was cut to fade from light to dark. 35½" x 56". *Courtesy Architectural Artifacts, Inc. Chicago.* $6300

Gorgeous floral design from Newark, N.J., c. 1895. *Courtesy of Richard Kurtz.* $2300

Victorian style window with flower pot design. 14" x 57". *Courtesy of Richard Kurtz.* $2995

Rippled opalescent with pressed jewel in the center. 32 x 33",
c. 1890s. *Courtesy of Bill Hylen.* $695

Right: Arched window with potted plant design and many
jewels of different sizes. 27" x 45". *Courtesy Paul Brown,
Red Baron's Antiques.*

Below: Transom window with floral design in opalescent glass.
43½" x 15½". *Courtesy Oley Valley Architectural Antiques.*
$795

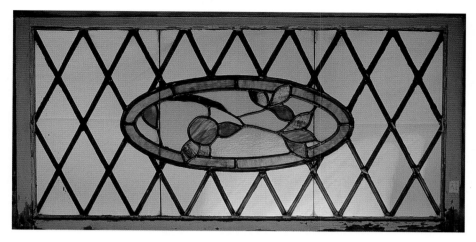

Apple design from Philadelphia. Opalescent glass, wide leading. Early 20th century. *Courtesy of Bill Hylen.* $395

Fruit bowl design with ripple and opalescent glass, jewels, and painted glass. From a house in Pasaic, New Jersey, c. 1890s. 55" x 27". *Courtesy of Bill Hylen.* $2995

Colorful window with many interesting pressed jewels. Several types of opalescent and ripple glass were used. 1880s-90s. 14½" x 43". *Courtesy of Richard Kurtz.* $2695

Rose design. Textured, cathedral, and opalescent glass.
24½" x 35" *Courtesy of Bill Hylen.* $395

Stained, painted, and jeweled landing window with lilies and dove.
54" x 93". *Courtesy Paul Brown, Red Baron's Antiques.*

Ornate window from Philadelphia, c. 1890s. 31" x 35".
Courtesy of Richard Kurtz. $3995

Urn. 17½" x 31". *Courtesy Oley Valley Architectural Antiques.* $495

Geometric design with fruit, c. 1925. 19½" x 25¾". *Courtesy of Richard Kurtz.* $500

Above: Intricate design with jewels and oval center. 28¾" x 27½". *Courtesy Oley Valley Architectural Antiques.* $1395

Above left: 1920s floral window with crackle and slag (darker opalescent) glass. Note the absence of jewels. 20" x 48".*Courtesy of Richard Kurtz.* $1795

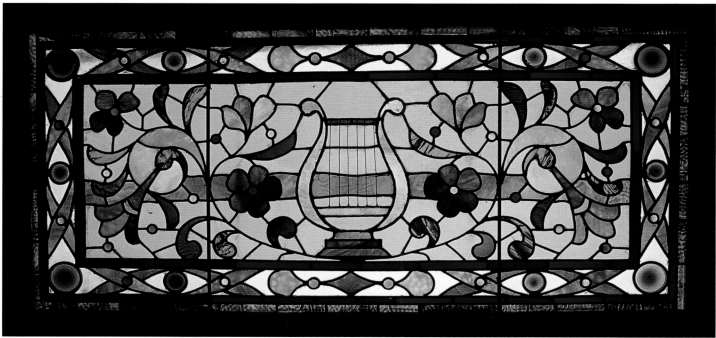

Victorian window with lyre image, c. 1890s. An array of glass types were used throughout the window. Note the symmetry of the design, and how both the jewels and glass alternate colors from one half of the design to the other. 44½" x 20". *Courtesy of Richard Kurtz.* $3500

Floral window from Newark, New Jersey, dating in the 1890s. The window has a great deal of amber crackle glass, as well as opalescent ripple. 52½" x 21½". *Courtesy of Richard Kurtz.* $3500

Fruit bowl. Includes ripple and opalescent glass, the most interesting of which is the pink and yellow opalescent of the interior. 1900-1910. 32" x 14". *Courtesy of Richard Kurtz.* $900

Door with vase and flower design. Pressed jewels, red flashed border. 21¾" x 36½". *Courtesy Oley Valley Architectural Antiques.* $1850

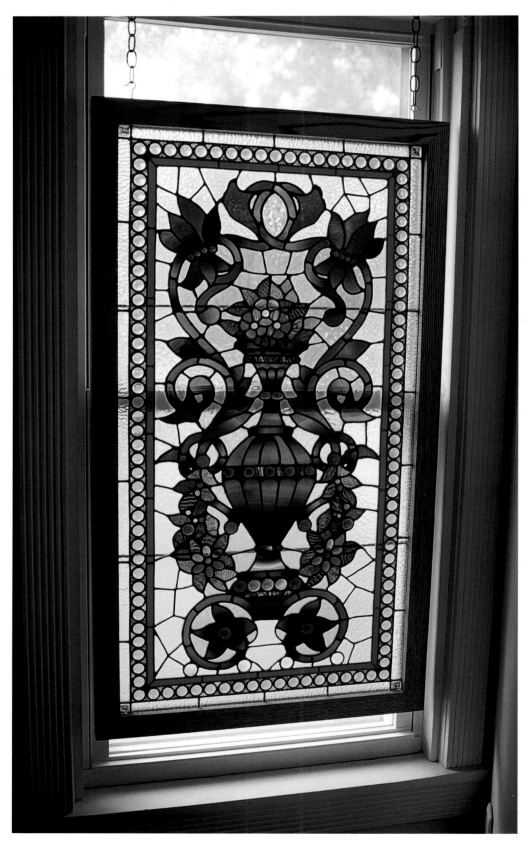

Vase design with many jewels and intricate cuts. Note the shading techniques used with the vase, leaves, and flowers. c. 1890s. *Courtesy of Richard Kurtz.* $7500

Floral garland design with fluted (top), glue chip (bottom), and ripple glass. Faceted jewels. 35" x 10½". *Courtesy of Bill Hylen.* $350.

American window with floral design, yellow background. 24½" x 37½". *Courtesy Architectural Artifacts, Inc. Chicago.* $1195

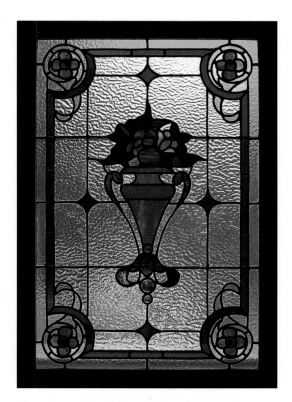

Vase design from Newark, New Jersey with intricate leadwork and many colors. c. 1900. *Courtesy of Richard Kurtz.* 23" x 32". $1500

Fruit garland. This window is made entirely of crackle glass and is in need of cleaning and repair. Note the shading effect on the garland the artist achieved with the glass. 44" x 18". 1890s. *Courtesy of Richard Kurtz.* $1200

American four-piece Art Nouveau landing window. Sides, 13½"w x 45½". Center, 25¼" x 49½". Transom, 67"w. *Courtesy Architectural Artifacts, Inc. Chicago.* $9900

Left: Art Noveau design with beveled glass in the center. 17½" x 13½". *Courtesy Hobbit Antiques.*

Rose arch. This is one of a group of at least ten identical windows that might have originally been designed to form an arch or even a full circle. The design includes ripple and opalescent glass. The manganese content in the clear glass has turned it a more purple hue. This window dates around the turn of the century. 14" x 9". *Courtesy of Richard Kurtz.* $175/Panel.

Two-panel landscape design with grapes. American cut glass. 21¼" x 57". *Courtesy Architectural Artifacts, Inc. Chicago.* $3800/Pair.

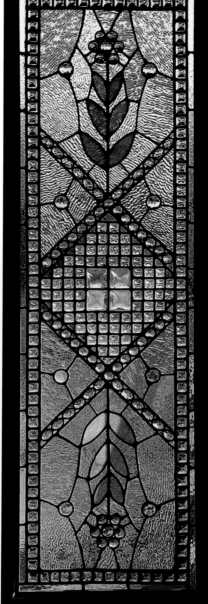

Combination window with geometric design in pinchback and faceted jewels. Background is lavender ripple glass. 15" x 52". $1895

Assymetrical floral design., c. 1880-90. 9¾" x 19¾". *Courtesy Oley Valley Architectural Antiques.* $340

Arts & Crafts design. Ripple and opalescent glass. *Courtesy of Bill Hylen.* $450

Numbered window in Arts & Crafts style. Hammered and opalescent glass. 1910-20. 60" x 23".
Courtesy of Bill Hylen. $395

Arts & Crafts design with rose. *Courtesy of Bill Hylen.* $250

Arts & Crafts rose. Hammered glass, rippled. 1910-1920.
24" x 16". *Courtesy of Bill Hylen.* $250 as is.

American Prairie School design with pink flower. 25¾" x 27¾". *Courtesy Architectural Artifacts, Inc. Chicago.* $425

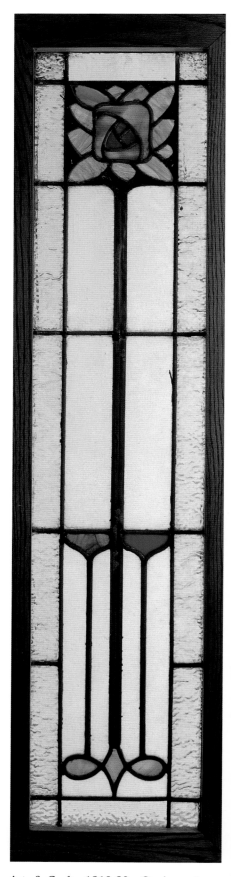

Arts & Crafts design with red poppies. 29¾" x 23¼". *Courtesy Oley Valley Architectural Antiques.* $795

Arts & Crafts, 1910-20s. Opalescent, ripple, and hammered glass. Very thick leading. 13½" x 47½" *Courtesy of Bill Hylen.* $695

Shield and wreath design on crackle glass background. 36" x 15½". *Courtesy Oley Valley Architectural Antiques.* $795

Victorian window with intricate leadwork and many small cuts of early opalescent glass. c. 1890s. 54" x 18" *Courtesy of Bill Hylen.* $1400

Fleur-de-lis design with opalescent glass. 24" x 46". *Courtesy Oley Valley Architectural Antiques.* $1495

Torch design with crackle and other textured glass. *Courtesy of Bill Hylen.* $450

Victorian design with jewel and textured glass. *Courtesy of Bill Hylen.* $395

Shield design with ribbons. 47½" x 15½". *Courtesy Oley Valley Architectural Antiques.* $795

Oval shield with green leaves. 43" x 19½". *Courtesy Oley Valley Architectural Antiques.* $695

Intricate Rudy Bros. landing window with griffin and shield design. 63" x 55". *Courtesy Paul Brown, Red Baron's Antiques.* $5500

Shield with jewels on a green opalescent background. 36" x 9". *Courtesy Oley Valley Architectural Antiques.* $795

Shield design with ribbons and pinchback jewels. 23¼" x 15¾". *Courtesy Architectural Artifacts, Inc. Chicago.* $1195

Matching pair of windows with many small cuts. The window on the left has over 130 pieces! c. 1890. Left, 26" x 12", $300. Above, 12" square, $200. *Courtesy of Bill Hylen.*

Window from a house designed by Philadelphia-area architect Frank Furness in Douglasville, Pennsylvania. The blue line running on the right edge of the window suggests that this window was actually a part of a larger configuration of windows. 18½" x 17½". *Courtesy Oley Valley Architectural Antiques.* $950

Torch design with clear glass, ripple glass, and small jewels. One of a pair, c. 1900. *Courtesy of Bill Hylen.* $1000/pair.

Clear window with torch design and jewel garland. 49½" x 27½". *Courtesy Oley Valley Architectural Antiques.* $1695

Wreath with fleur-de-lis. Note the jewel flowers and the red glass used to fill in the spaces between the petals. 61½" x 16" *Courtesy Oley Valley Architectural Antiques.* $1195

Shield design with many colored, textured glasses and faceted jewels. 42" x 18½". *Courtesy Oley Valley Architectural Antiques.* $850

Colorful window with jewels, opalescent, and textured glasses. Shell and swag design. 28" x 19¾". *Courtesy Hobbit Antiques.* $995

Wreath with blue ribbon and small jewels. 47" x 15". *Courtesy Oley Valley Architectural Antiques.* $750

"Three dimensional" window with many chunk jewels throughout the border and central design. 1890s. 30" x 16". *Courtesy of Richard Kurtz.* $3000

Urn with swags. 60" x 24½". *Courtesy Oley Valley Architectural Antiques.* $1995

Torches and flowers. Intricate window with many small cuts and types of glass. Note the early opalescent ripple glass at the center that fades through several shades of pink. 1890s. 13½" x 29". *Courtesy of Richard Kurtz.* $1150

Window with shield design from a house in Newark, New Jersey, c. 1890. One of a pair. 22" x 26". *Courtesy of Richard Kurtz.* $4000/Pair.

Urn with opalescent ribbon. 40" x 13". *Courtesy Oley Valley Architectural Antiques.* $795

Wreath design with intricate cuts. Opalescent, hammered, and textured glass. *Courtesy of Bill Hylen.* $500

Arch design with shield and intertwining ribbons on blue background. 27½" x 35". *Courtesy Oley Valley Architectural Antiques.* $495

Wreath and torch design from Newark, New Jersey, c. 1895. *Courtesy of Richard Kurtz.* $1800

Fleur-de-lis and ribbon design in opalescent glass. 40½" x 11½". *Courtesy Oley Valley Architectural Antiques.* $595

Stained and jeweled window with oil lamp and fleur-de-lis design. 60" x 46". *Courtesy Paul Brown, Red Baron's Antiques.* $2995

Fleur-de-lis with jewels. 47½" x 28¾". *Courtesy Oley Valley Architectural Antiques.* $1295

Large turn-of-the-century window from Minnesota. Central design has beveled glass with a zipper cut. Ripple, opalescent, and art glass. 26" x 49". *Courtesy of Richard Kurtz.* $6500

Top half of a double-hung window. 23½" x 30". *Courtesy Oley Valley Architectural Antiques.* $595

Flower and shield design. The yellow opalescent glass surrounding the central image is difficult to come by today, which will make repairing the breaks much more of a challenge. 39" x 12½". 1920s. *Courtesy of Richard Kurtz.* As is, $150.

Rectangular design in opalescent glass with swags. 53½" x 15". *Courtesy Oley Valley Architectural Antiques.* $595

Window from New Jersey. Torch design with opalescent jewels. 1920s. *Courtesy of Richard Kurtz.* 18½" x 56". $550

Very intricate design with ripple and older opalescent glass. One of a pair. 14½" x 22". *Courtesy of Bill Hylen.* $750/Pair.

Torch design with pink flames and graduated jewel garland. 42" x 14". *Courtesy Oley Valley Architectural Antiques.* $1195

Shield design with ribbons, jewels, and roundels on a fluted glass background. 42" x 33¼". *Courtesy Oley Valley Architectural Antiques.* $1295

Top half of a double-hung window, c. 1900. 28½" x 23½" *Courtesy of Bill Hylen.* $200

Three-part landing window with torch design on lower panels and a Victorian flourish on the arch. 56" x 81" overall. *Courtesy Paul Brown, Red Baron's Antiques.* $4995

Fluted glass with colored center. Note how the cuts were arranged so that the texture of the fluting adds another dimension to the design. 33" x 12" *Courtesy Oley Valley Architectural Antiques.* $495

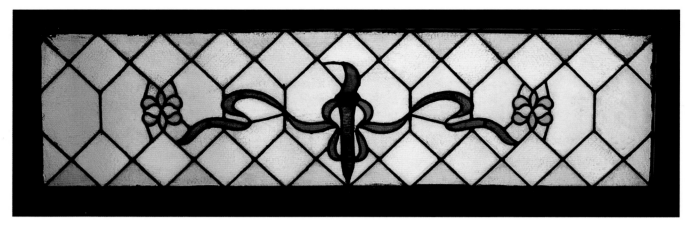

Torch with ribbons on harlequin background. 43¾" x 12". *Courtesy Oley Valley Architectural Antiques.* $495

Wreath design, 43" x 23½". *Courtesy Oley Valley Architectural Antiques.* $995

Fleur-de-lis design in opalescent glass, c. 1900. 21½" x 45½". *Courtesy of Bill Hylen.* $600.

Interesting shades of opalescent glass, with two red jewels. 50" x 39". *Courtesy Oley Valley Architectural Antiques.* $650

Shell design in oval. 29½" x 27½". *Courtesy Oley Valley Architectural Antiques.* $550

Intricate "three-dimensional" window dating around 1890. The flowers are all made of chunk jewels. 39" x 11". *Courtesy of Richard Kurtz.* $3500 as is.

Shield design from the Glasgow, School. 25" x 20". *Courtesy Architectural Artifacts, Inc. Chicago.* $465

Geometric shield design. Hammered and opalescent glass. 27½" x 30". *Courtesy of Bill Hylen.* $300

Chapter Two
Arches & Round Windows

Arched transom with rectangular jewels, crackle, and beveled glass. 57½"w x 23½"h. *Courtesy Architectural Artifacts, Inc. Chicago.* $1995

Arch with fleur-de-lis, blue border. 61" x 13". *Courtesy of Bill Hylen.* $650.

Arch window with many small pieces and small jewels, c. 1890s. 48" x 21½". *Courtesy of Bill Hylen.* $1500

American arch window, brown with jewels. Circles with Celtic knots. 75½" x 38". *Courtesy Architectural Artifacts, Inc. Chicago.* $2595

Philadelphia window, very common design with fluted, textured, and opalescent glass and jewels, c. 1900. 32" x 27". *Courtesy of Bill Hylen.* $595.

Daisy design with ripple glass. 14" x 15½". *Courtesy Oley Valley Architectural Antiques.* $295

Arch-shaped window with jewels, ripple glass, and opalescent ripple glass. 63" x 19". *Courtesy of Bill Hylen.* 1890s. $2350

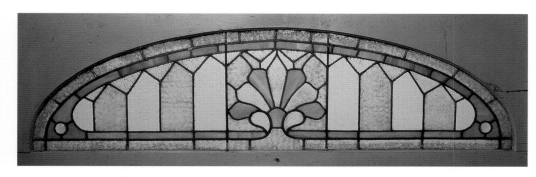

Arch with opalescent and textured glass, and two large jewels, c. 1900. *Courtesy of Bill Hylen.* $600

Arched transom with shell at top. 52½" x 16". *Courtesy Architectural Artifacts, Inc. Chicago.* $2350

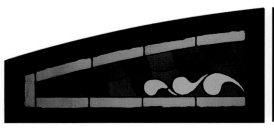

Three-piece set with interesting roundel in center. Center, 25½" x 11", sides 25" x 9" each. *Courtesy Oley Valley Architectural Antiques.* $795

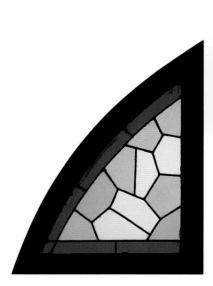

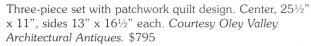

Three-piece set with patchwork quilt design. Center, 25½" x 11", sides 13" x 16½" each. *Courtesy Oley Valley Architectural Antiques.* $795

Floral design in rich opalescent hues. 27" x 11". *Courtesy Oley Valley Architectural Antiques.* $595

Arched transom. 33½" x 14". *Courtesy Oley Valley Architectural Antiques.* $595

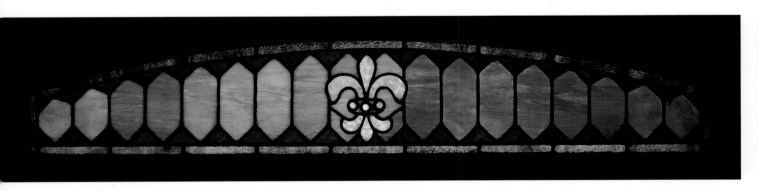

Arched transom with fleur-de-lis. 55" x 9½". *Courtesy Oley Valley Architectural Antiques.* $795

American arched designs with beveled glass and jewels. These windows have an interesting partial symmetry. 69" x 30½". *Courtesy Architectural Artifacts, Inc. Chicago.* $1995 each.

Colorful arch with patchwork design in various textures and jewels. 56" x 21". *Courtesy Oley Valley Architectural Antiques.* $1895

Ornate design with hammered, ripple, and glue chip glass. 24½" x 23¾". *Courtesy Oley Valley Architectural Antiques.* $695

Victorian window with opalescent glass and pressed jewels. One of a pair. 29" x 24". *Courtesy of Bill Hylen.* $395

Arched transom with shield design on fluted glass background. 41" x 25¼". *Courtesy Oley Valley Architectural Antiques.* $1495

Simple arched design in cathedral and opalescent glass. 29" x 19". *Courtesy of Bill Hylen.* $300

Arched two-part window with flower design. 31½" x 69". *Courtesy Architectural Artifacts, Inc. Chicago.* $2995

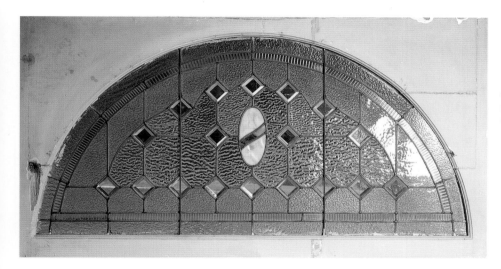

Arched window with beveled and textured glasses, c. 1890. 49" x 23½". *Courtesy Oley Valley Architectural Antiques.* $950

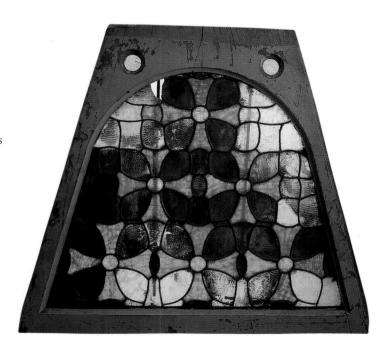

Most of this arched window is plated on the back to create a double layer. The dark colors come from the back layer, and there is clear ripple glass on top, as shown in the areas that are missing the plate. 44" (bottom) x 39" high. *Courtesy of Bill Hylen.* $400 as is, $750 restored.

Arch design. c. 1890. 57" x 16". *Courtesy of Bill Hylen.* $300 as is, $600 restored.

Gothic arch with sunburst design. 33" x 47½". *Courtesy Oley Valley Architectural Antiques.* $795

Gothic arch with several jewels and colored glasses, including mottled red oxblood glass. 51" x 64". *Courtesy Oley Valley Architectural Antiques.* $2000

Wagon wheel frame with unusual stained glass design. Usually a frame like this would have solid panes. c. 1900. 32" x 18". *Courtesy of Bill Hylen.* $400

Arched design with relief leadwork and clear background. *Courtesy Oley Valley Architectural Antiques.* $1495 ea.

Arch design in ripple and opalescent glass, c. 1890s. This window is almost entirely releaded. $750

Arched transom with oplaescent glass. 63" x 14½". *Courtesy Oley Valley Architectural Antiques.* $1195

Arched transom with Arts & Crafts floral design. 53" x 12¾". *Courtesy Oley Valley Architectural Antiques.* $950

This window has very thin leading, small jewels, and hand-cut chunk jewels in the leading of the vase. Several of the panels have been replaced. c. 1890s. 53" x 19". *Courtesy of Bill Hylen.* $2500

Transom window. 27½" x 11". *Courtesy Oley Valley Architectural Antiques.* $540

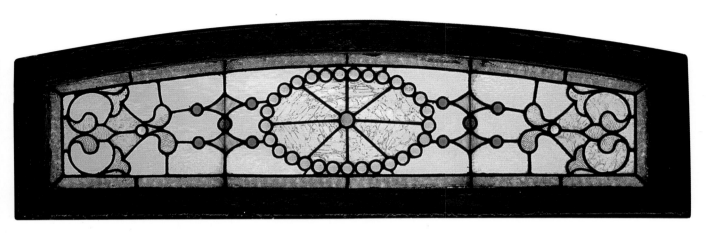

Arch design, ripple and crackle glass with vaseline glass jewels, c.1890s. 48" x 14". *Courtesy of Bill Hylen.*
$850

Arched design with jewels and fluted glass. 41¾" x 25½". *Courtesy Oley Valley Architectural Antiques.*
$1295

Arched transom, unframed. Note how the glass on the red flowers was cut to fade to white. 41" x 18½".
Courtesy Architectural Artifacts, Inc. Chicago. $650

Ceiling panel, very fine leadwork. 27" square. *Courtesy of Bill Hylen.* $775

Round window with white opalescent glass, colorful jewels, thick leading, and ornate applied leading. 21½" diameter. *Courtesy Oley Valley Architectural Antiques.* $895

Round design with opalescent jewels. 19¾"diameter. *Courtesy Architectural Artifacts, Inc. Chicago.* $850

Oval window. Opalescent and ripple glass, with central design made of amber pinchback jewels. 17" x 27". *Courtesy Hobbit Antiques.* $995

Four-lobed geometric design in pastel shades of opalescent glass. 31½" diameter. *Courtesy Hobbit Antiques.* $795

Ornate design in opalescent glass. 46½" diameter. *Courtesy Oley Valley Architectural Antiques.* $4500

Round window with opalescent glass. 25½" diameter. *Courtesy Oley Valley Architectural Antiques.* $795

Large round ceiling light, Victorian design with ripple glass and jewels. 144" diameter. *Courtesy Paul Brown, Red Baron's Antiques.*

Chapter 3

Designs in Clear Glass

Doors from a home in Philadelphia, c. 1880. crackle glass is used in the central designs. 13½" x 63" in oak frame. *Courtesy Oley Valley Architectural Antiques.* $5500 pr.

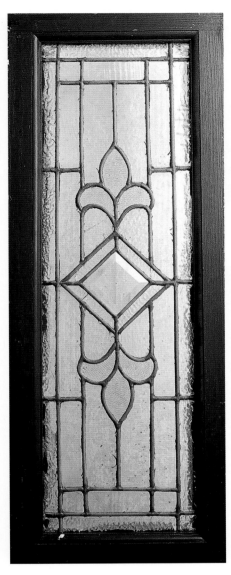

Shield design with textured and fluted glass, square jewels. 34½" x 12". *Courtesy Oley Valley Architectural Antiques.* $495

Beveled center with ripple and fluted glass, c. 1910. 9" x 32". *Courtesy of Bill Hylen.* $300

American beveled window with zinc caming. 42½" x 31". *Courtesy Architectural Artifacts, Inc. Chicago.* $1295

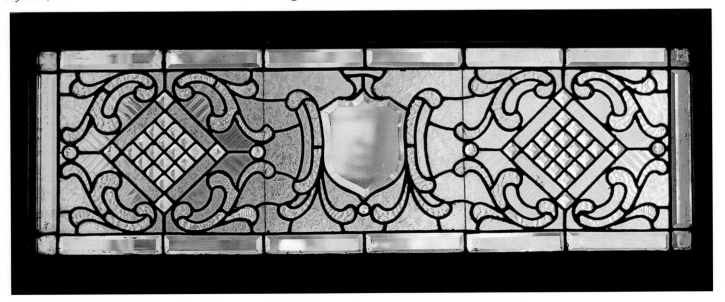

Intricate Philadelphia window, c. 1900. There is a great variety of clear glass, including beveled, double glue chip, and fluted glass. 35" x 11". *Courtesy of Richard Kurtz.* $1400

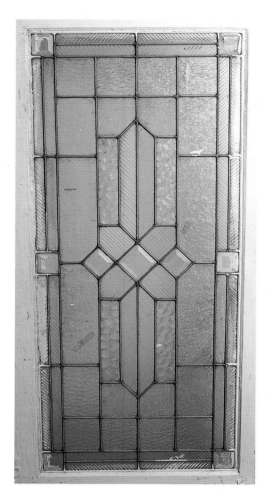

Four-petal flower design with textured and fluted glass. 26½" x 19½". *Courtesy Oley Valley Architectural Antiques.* $495

Rondells, fluted and other textured glass, c.1900. *Courtesy of Bill Hylen.* $250

Beveled design with etched center. 29" x 13". *Courtesy Oley Valley Architectural Antiques.* $695

Asymmetrical two-part window with many textures of clear glass. 1890-1900. Top half, 36½" x 36½". Bottom half, 36½" x 36½". *Courtesy of Bill Hylen.* $2500/pair.

Clear window with many pieces of ripple glass. 1920s. 23" x 34". *Courtesy of Bill Hylen.* $150

Beveled and glue chip glass. 26¼" x 26¾". *Courtesy Architectural Artifacts, Inc. Chicago.* $425

Shield design with fluted and glue chip glass in background. 40¾" x 13½". *Courtesy Oley Valley Architectural Antiques.* $595

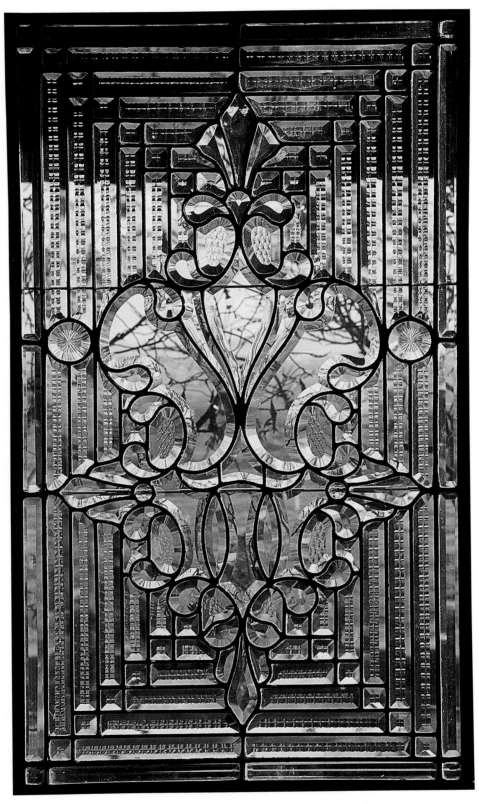

Intricate design with beveled glass. Note zipper cuts in the straight panes. 24" x 42".
Courtesy Hobbit Antiques. $1995

Fluted, granite, and textured glass, c. 1880. 23" x 31". *Courtesy Oley Valley Architectural Antiques.* $495

Textured and beveled glass. 25" x 34". *Courtesy Oley Valley Architectural Antiques.* $550

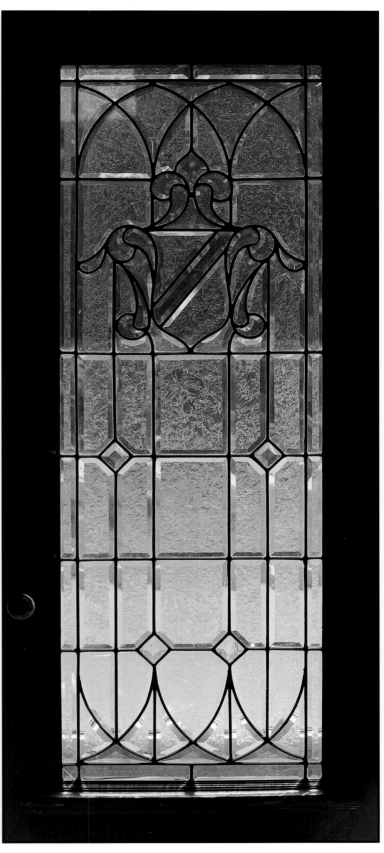

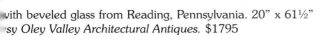
...with beveled glass from Reading, Pennsylvania. 20" x 61½"
...sy *Oley Valley Architectural Antiques.* $1795

Door with shield design and beveled glue chip glass. 20½" x 59".
Courtesy Oley Valley Architectural Antiques. $1795

Door with beveled glue chip glass, oval design in center.
47½". *Courtesy Oley Valley Architectural Antiques.* $28

Door with beveled glass. 18" x 52". *Courtesy Oley Valley Architectural Antiques.* $1395

Door with beveled glue chip glass. Etched center. 18½" x 59".
Courtesy Oley Valley Architectural Antiques. $1795

Sidelight with beveled and glue chip glass. 7½" x 59½".
Courtesy Oley Valley Architectural Antiques. $550

Asymmetrical design with beveled glass, zipper cuts, and jewels. 49¾" x 18". *Courtesy Architectural Artifacts, Inc. Chicago.* $1295

Transom window, beveled glass, etched center. Note the top corners are curved. 29½" x 13". *Courtesy Oley Valley Architectural Antiques.* $695

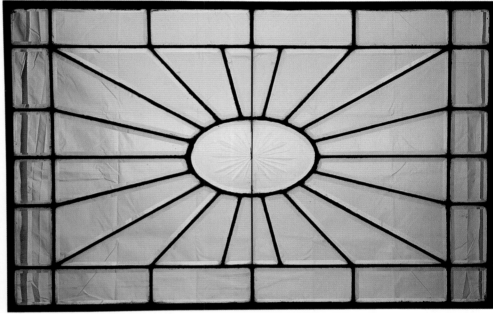

Window from a house in Scranton, Pennsylvania, c. 1930.
Etched center, various textured glass. *Courtesy of Bill Hylen.*
$495

Beveled glass with wheel-cut starburst design. *Courtesy Architectural Artifacts, Inc. Chicago.* $1200

Curved bevels, zinc leading, etching. 49" x 17". *Courtesy of Bill Hylen.* $995

Beveled fleur-de-lis design with zipper cuts. 29" x 14". *Courtesy Architectural Artifacts, Inc. Chicago.* $1195

American design with zinc border and raised lead rosettes. 31¾" x 27¼". *Courtesy Architectural Artifacts, Inc. Chicago.* $895

Spider web design in beveled glass. 53" x 25½". *Courtesy Hobbit Antiques.* $1195

Clear sidelight with etched glass in center and large jewels that might have been added to the window. Set of two. 9½" x 63". *Courtesy of Bill Hylen.* $595

Torch design with crackle, fluted, and other textured glass, and vaseline glass jewels. One of a pair. 22" x 48". *Courtesy of Bill Hylen.* $1500/pair.

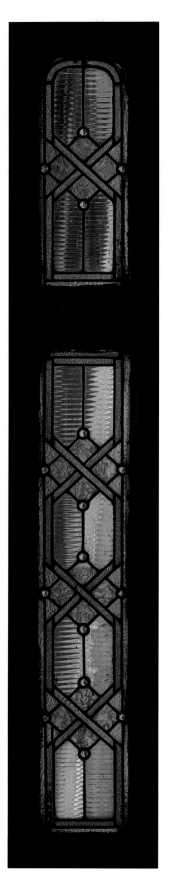

Clear sidelight with fluted and glue chip glass Top panel, 8" x 19¾". Bottom panel, 8" x 39¾". *Courtesy Oley Valley Architectural Antiques.* $595/pair.

Fluted and rippled glass with jewels and beveled center. c. 1900. 16" x 42". *Courtesy of Bill Hylen.* $600

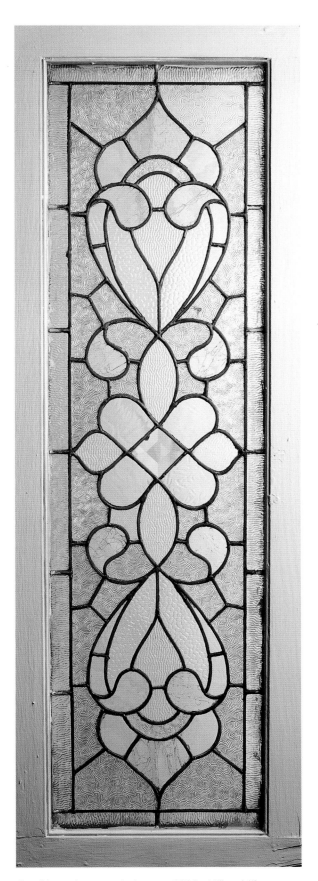

Crackle and textured glass. c. 1900. 15" x 44".
Courtesy of Bill Hylen. $600

Beveled and textured glass, pressed roundels. 13" x 41½".
Courtesy Oley Valley Architectural Antiques. $595

Beveled glue chip glass. 45" x 17". *Courtesy Hobbit Antiques.* $795

Window from Detroit, Michigan, c. 1890. Note the bevels around the flowers.
19" x 25½". *Courtesy of Richard Kurtz.* $1500/Pair.

Asymmetrical design with beveled glass and faceted jewels. 10½" x 30¾". *Courtesy Architectural Artifacts, Inc. Chicago.* $895

Beveled, textured, fluted, and textured glass. c. 1920s. *Courtesy of Bill Hylen.* $250

135

Beveled glass, 31½" x 15½". *Courtesy Hobbit Antiques.* $995 pr.

American window, beveled and jeweled. 24" x 61". *Courtesy Architectural Artifacts, Inc. Chicago.* $3200

Ornate design with textured glass, somewhat tinted by manganese. 40" x 24". *Courtesy Oley Valley Architectural Antiques.* $895

Crackle, fluted, and other textured glass with jewels and beveled center. Buckled. 32" x 40". 1900-1910. *Courtesy of Bill Hylen.* $400

Square prairie style design, beveled. 17¼" sq. *Courtesy Architectural Artifacts, Inc. Chicago.* $550

Beveled and textured clear glass, Art Deco design. 54½" x 11½". *Courtesy Hobbit Antiques.*

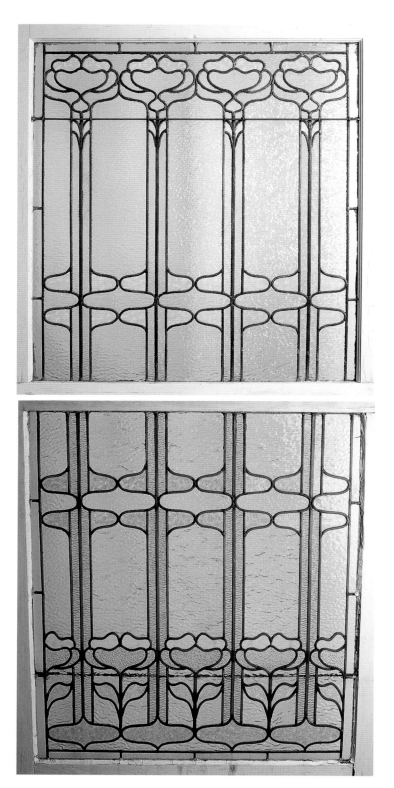

Two-part Arts & Crafts design. Lavender tint from the aging manganese in the glass. Many textures. Each measures 32" x 34". *Courtesy of Bill Hylen.* $1000/pair.

Arts & Crafts design with various textured glass. *Courtesy of Bill Hylen.* $200

English Arts & Crafts design. 39" x 26". *Courtesy Architectural Artifacts, Inc. Chicago.* $625

Chapter Four
Painted & Etched Windows
Painted Windows

Fired-on paint and colored glass. 54" x 29½" *Courtesy Oley Valley Architectural Antiques.* $1195

Octagonal church window, painted lyre design, in new frame. 18" diameter. *Courtesy of Bill Hylen.* $650

English reverse-painted bird and foliage. 18¾" x 29¼". *Courtesy Architectural Artifacts, Inc. Chicago.* $695

English reverse-painted art glass window with birds and flowers. 19" x 29¾". *Courtesy Architectural Artifacts, Inc. Chicago.* $695

Patchwork quilt style transom window with bird painted in center. 27" x 9½". *Courtesy Oley Valley Architectural Antiques.* $695

Arch with owl painting and patchwork background. Ripple and other textured glass, jewels. 48" x 21". *Courtesy of Bill Hylen.* $895

142

Painted face from a theater in Minneapolis. 59" x 34½". *Courtesy Architectural Artifacts, Inc. Chicago.* $2200

Painted wreath and torch in circle, with background in opalescent glass. 35½" x 19". *Courtesy Oley Valley Architectural Antiques.* $695

Interesting turn-of-the-century window, possibly English. Enchanced with roundels and painted designs. Look closely at the bird image in the lower half; the design was acid-etched into red flash glass and then painted. 18" x 30". *Courtesy of Richard Kurtz.* $1495

Transom window with birds painted in the center. The window was made with cathedral glass, although red and royal blue were the most expensive colors. c. 1890. 47" x 17". *Courtesy of Bill Hylen.* $975

Painted window, "To Thee All Angels Cry Aloud." One of four. 31½" x 66½". *Courtesy Oley Valley Architectural Antiques.* $4995 ea.

Painted metal casement window with urn and floral design. 42" x 95".
Courtesy Paul Brown, Red Baron's Antiques.

These images came from a large clear window with a border of smaller windows. The designs include red and royal blue flash glass, roundels, jewels, and painting. The original window was located in a funeral home built in the late 1880s. Each panel measures 12½" x 12½". *Courtesy of Bill Hylen.* $400 each.

Right: Several panels like this one separated the head windows, which were in the corners. The design includes painting and roundels. 12½" x 12½". *Courtesy of Bill Hylen.* $275 each.

American oval-shaped window, painted and leaded with birds and nest, jewels. 26½" x 48½".
Courtesy Architectural Artifacts, Inc. Chicago. $4800

Painted window from a house in Philadelphia, c. 1885. 25" x 21". *Courtesy of Bill Hylen.* $775.

Painted clear glass window that reads "Lifting better up to best." It could have possibly come from a school. The leading is buckling, and several panels are cracked. *Courtesy of Bill Hylen.* Restored, $750.

Painted window from Philadelphia. The top is arched, and the window is still in its original peg frame. The detailed painted design is surrounded by pinch-back jewels. 1890s. 26" x 43½" *Courtesy of Richard Kurtz.* $3500

Glasgow School Arts & Crafts design. 15¼" x 29¼". *Courtesy Architectural Artifacts, Inc. Chicago.* $465

Screen with copper caming. 15¾" x 23¼". *Courtesy Architectural Artifacts, Inc. Chicago.* $1795

English Arts & Crafts design, painted. 23¼"w x 27¼". *Courtesy Architectural Artifacts, Inc. Chicago.* $895

English Art Nouveau design, painted. 27" x 37½". *Courtesy Architectural Artifacts, Inc. Chicago.* $975

American etched window with nine panes, in red and blue flashed glass. 18" x 20½". *Courtesy Architectural Artifacts, Inc. Chicago.* $375

Etched glass window, c. 1920s. 14½" x 54". *Courtesy of Bill Hylen.* $400

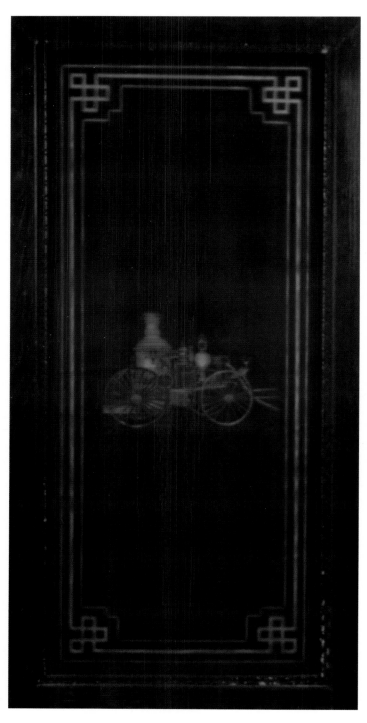

Etched window originally from a fire station door, picturing an old pumper, c. 1870s. *Courtesy of James and Sandra Piatti.* $495

Flashed glass, wheel-etched by hand, c. 1880s. 10" x 34". *Courtesy of Bill Hylen.* $195

Flashed, glue chip, and etched glass. All of these techniques were executed on the same piece of glass; in what order was this design made? One of a pair of doors that were in a row house in North Philadelphia. 12½" x 37". *Courtesy of Bill Hylen.* $1000 for both doors.

English "Surgery" sign, etched on red flashed glass. 43½" x 9". *Courtesy Architectural Artifacts, Inc. Chicago.* $895

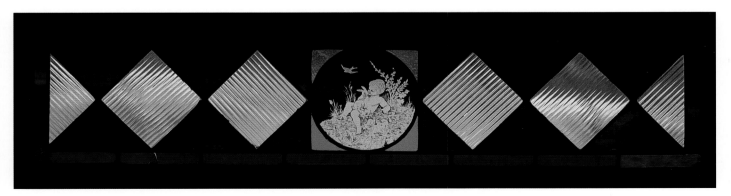

Flashed and fluted glass, with an etched central image of a child and rabbits. 56½" x 12". *Courtesy Oley Valley Architectural Antiques.* $695

Chapter Five
A Touch of Glass: Gallery of Manchester Windows

Another type of window you will frequently encounter in the antiques marketplace is smaller, mass-produced English windows. These windows usually feature a central design in colored glass on a background field of clear textured glass. Prices for these windows often fall between $50 and $250, depending on the intricacy of the design and where you find them. They make beautiful decorative accents throughout the home, and their size allows them to be hung easily just about anywhere. The wide diversity of colors and designs, combined with their current value and availablity, make these windows quite collectible. Be warned that time is of the essence; like all antique decorative windows, these are disappearing quickly! *Windows on pages 159-177 appear courtesy of Architectural Artifacts, Inc., Chicago.*

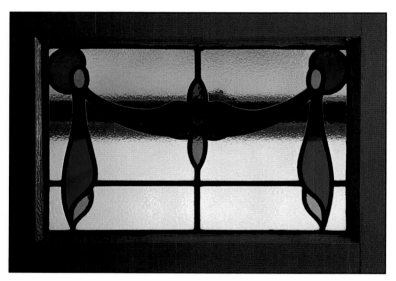

16½" x 11". *Courtesy of M. Wayne and JoAnn C. Etzweiler.* $85

16½" x 12½". *Courtesy of M. Wayne and JoAnn C. Etzweiler.* $50

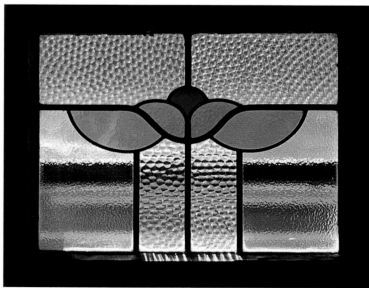

16½" x 15". *Courtesy of M. Wayne and JoAnn C. Etzweiler.* $40

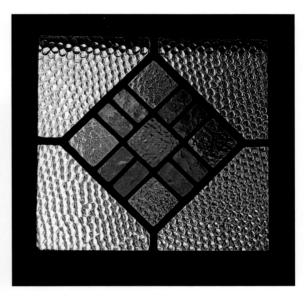

12" x 11½". *Courtesy of M. Wayne and JoAnn C. Etzweiler.* $50

20½" x 13½". *Courtesy of M. Wayne and JoAnn C. Etzweiler.* $50

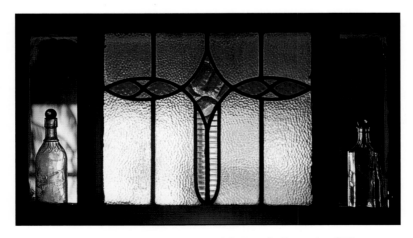

17" x 14½". *Courtesy of M. Wayne and JoAnn C. Etzweiler.* $75

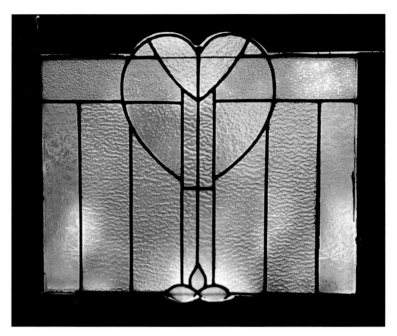

19" x 14½". *Courtesy of M. Wayne and JoAnn C. Etzweiler.* $65

16" x 16". *Courtesy of M. Wayne and JoAnn C. Etzweiler.* $50

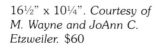

16½" x 10¼". *Courtesy of M. Wayne and JoAnn C. Etzweiler.* $60

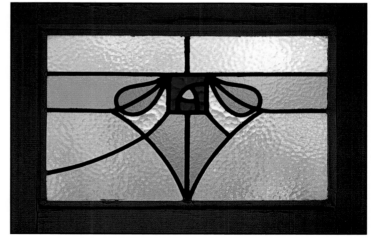

$40

$50

$40

$50

$50

$50

$40

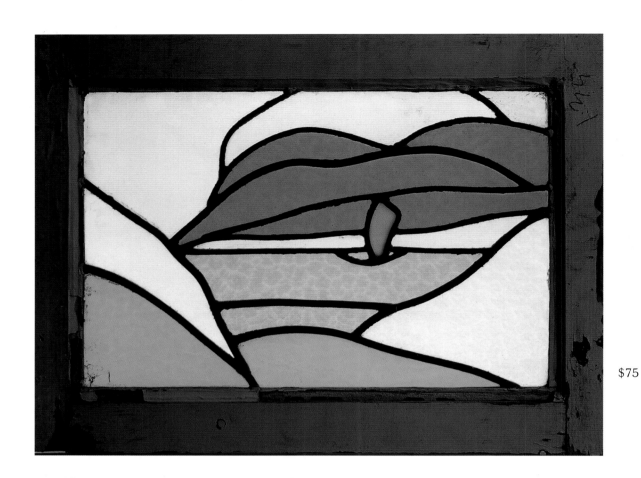

$75

$50

$75

$40

$40

$40

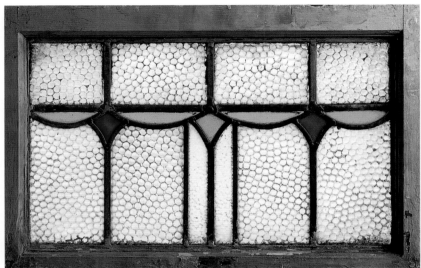

$45

$60

164

$65

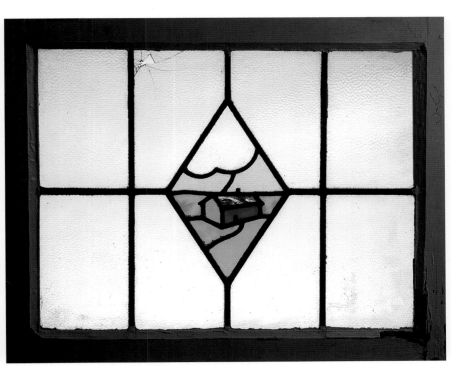

$65

$40

$50

$40

$40

$50

166

$150

$95

$95

$50

$60

$40

$50

$40

$50

$40

169

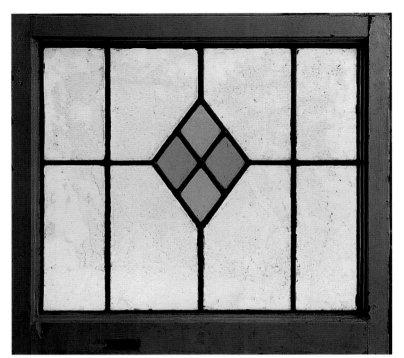

$35

$45

$35

$45

$35

$40

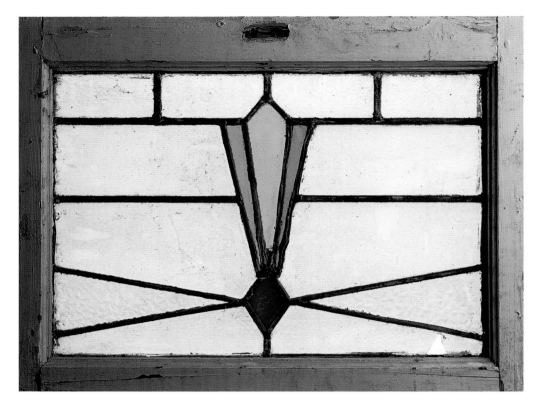

$45

$95

$45

$45

$40

$40

$40

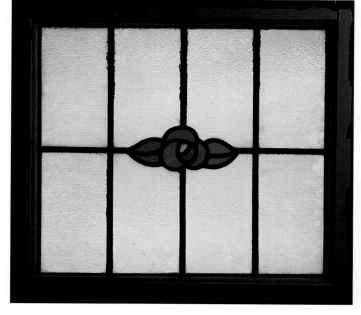

$45

$40

174

$40

$40

$40

$75

$90

Bibliography

Anscombe, Isabel. *Arts & Crafts Style.* London: Phaidon Press, Ltd., 1991.

Frueh, Ernie R. and Florence. *Chicago Stained Glass.* (Chicago: Wild Onion Books, 1998.)

Dorothy L. Maddy, Barbara E. Kreuger, and Richard L. Hoover, eds. *SGAA Reference and Technical Manual.* (Lee's Summit, MO: Stained Glass Association of America, 1992.)

Sittenfield, Michael, ed. *The Prairie School: Design Vision for the Midwest.* Vol. 21, no. 2 of *The Art Institute of Chicago Museum Studies,* 1995.

Wilson, H. Weber. *Great Glass in American Architecture.* New York: E.P. Dutton, 1986.

Appendix
Stained Glass Catalogs

The designs shown in this book are only as suggestions for help in buying. The detail can be more or less elaborate, the material made of a dozen kinds of glass, the colors varied to suit any plan of decoration. Special designs submitted when desired.

Prices given are the usual ones for the treatment as shown. Should it be desired to spend more or less advise us and the work can be modified accordingly.

Whatever the cost, the material and work will be good and care taken to secure harmony of color and design.

Cleveland Window Glass Co

Suggestions for Ordering

Be explicit, do not assume that we know what is wanted.

In specifying sizes always give width first.

Always give number of design wanted.

We assume you have reference to this catalogue in the absence of other instructions. While we endeavor to match the shades in the glass shown in the designs, it is not always possible owing to variation in the glass.

The first catalog is from the Cleveland Window Glass Company, c. 1900, and is pictured here in its entirety. It features a diverse assortment of windows, some quite elaborate. The number and complexity of standard designs offered by the company (in addition to the company's offer of custom design work) suggests that decorative windows were regularly included in contemporary buildings.

The second group of catalog images are taken from the *Pacific Northwest Millwork Catalog* of the City Planing Mill Company of Portland Oregon. The catalog dates 1927 and shows a far simpler assortment of window designs, suggesting less of a demand for ornate decorative windows as the twentieth century progressed.

516     $1.75 per sq ft

523     $1.60 per sq ft

528     $1.40 per sq ft

535     $1.50 per sq ft

532   $1.20 per sq ft

540     $1.25 per sq ft

542     $1.60 per sq ft

545     $1.60 per sq ft

560     $1.25 per sq ft

Leaded Art Glass Colored

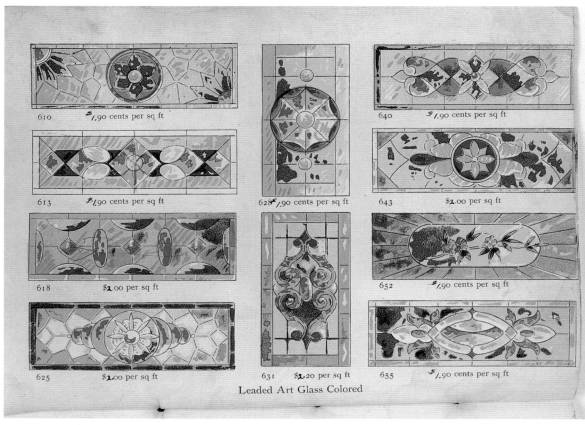

610     $1.90 cents per sq ft

640     $1.90 cents per sq ft

613     $1.90 cents per sq ft

628   $1.90 cents per sq ft

643     $2.00 per sq ft

618     $2.00 per sq ft

652     $1.90 cents per sq ft

625     $2.00 per sq ft

631     $1.20 per sq ft

655     $1.90 cents per sq ft

Leaded Art Glass Colored

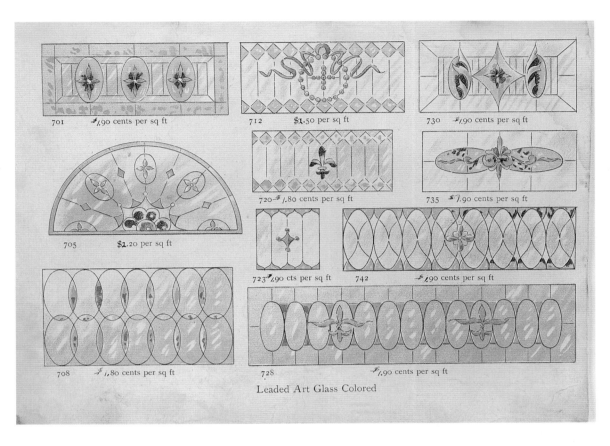

701     $1.90 cents per sq ft
712     $1.50 per sq ft
730     $1.90 cents per sq ft
720     $1.80 cents per sq ft
735     $1.90 cents per sq ft
705     $1.20 per sq ft
723     $1.90 cts per sq ft
742     $1.90 cents per sq ft
708     $1.80 cents per sq ft
728     $1.90 cents per sq ft

Leaded Art Glass Colored

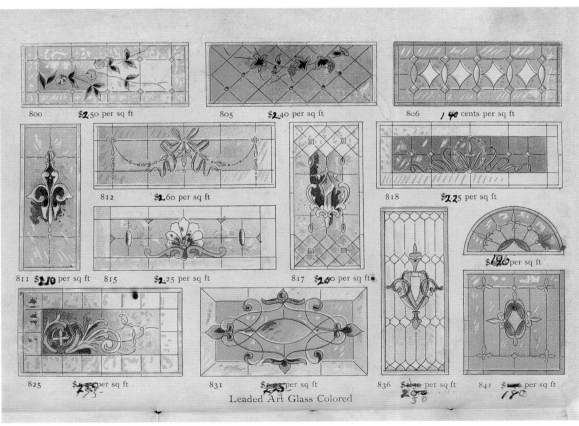

800     $2.50 per sq ft
805     $2.40 per sq ft
806     $1.40 cents per sq ft
812     $1.60 per sq ft
818     $2.25 per sq ft
811     $2.10 per sq ft
815     $2.25 per sq ft
817     $2.00 per sq ft
$1.95 per sq ft
825     $1.75 per sq ft
831     $2.50 per sq ft
836     $2.00 30 per sq ft
841     $1.70 per sq ft

Leaded Art Glass Colored

181

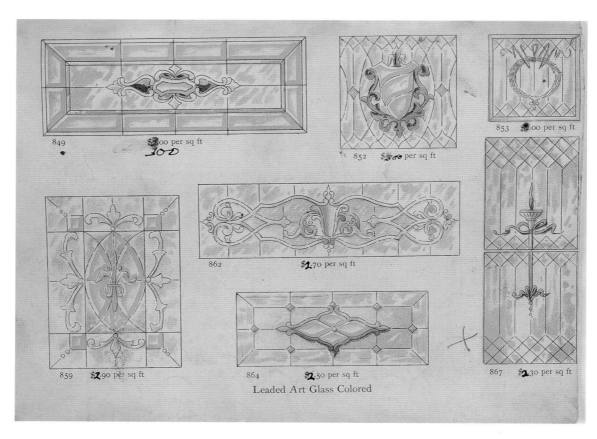

849      $3.00 per sq ft

300

852      $3.00 per sq ft

853      $3.00 per sq ft

862      $2.70 per sq ft

859      $2.90 per sq ft

864      $2.50 per sq ft

867      $2.30 per sq ft

Leaded Art Glass Colored

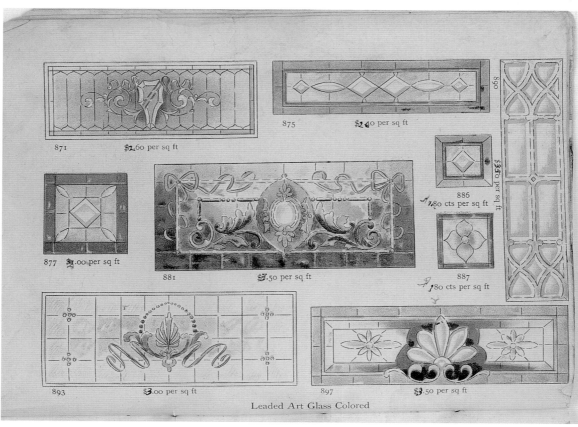

871      $2.60 per sq ft

875      $2.40 per sq ft

890

886      $1.80 cts per sq ft

$3.30 per sq ft

877      $2.00 per sq ft

881      $3.50 per sq ft

887      $1.80 cts per sq ft

893      $3.00 per sq ft

897      $3.50 per sq ft

Leaded Art Glass Colored

902     $1.60 per sq ft

905     $1.80 per sq ft

906     $1.80 per sq ft

910     $3.75 per sq ft

913     $3.20 per sq ft

916     $1.80 per sq ft

920   2.80 per sq ft

923     $2.50 per sq ft

924     $4.00 per sq ft

Leaded Art Glass Colored

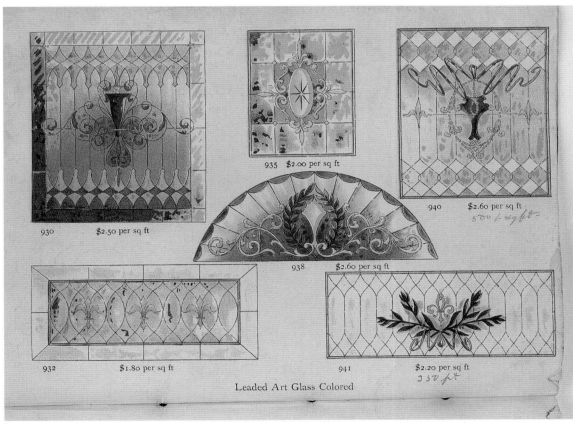

930     $2.50 per sq ft

932     $1.80 per sq ft

935     $2.00 per sq ft

938     $2.60 per sq ft

940     $2.60 per sq ft

941     $2.20 per sq ft

Leaded Art Glass Colored

944     $1.60 per sq ft

951     $2.50 per sq ft

955     $2.60 per sq ft

950     $2.00 per sq ft

947     $1.60 per sq ft

958     $2.00 per sq ft

Leaded Art Glass Colored

960     $2.00 per sq ft

963     $1.60 per sq ft

966     $1.50 per sq ft

973     $1.80 per sq ft

968     $2.00 per sq ft

976     $1.60 per sq ft

970     $1.25 per sq ft

974     $1.50 per sq ft

979     $2.50 per sq ft

Leaded Art Glass Colored

184

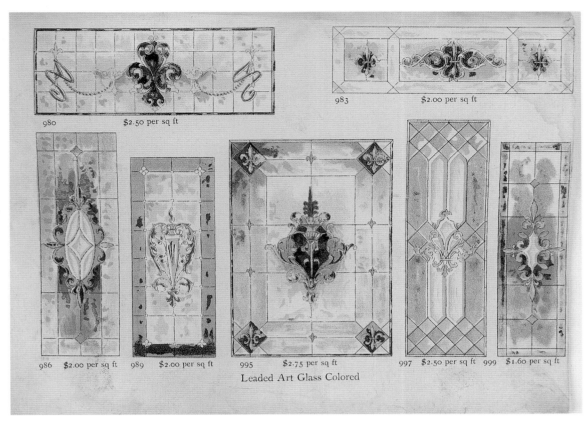

980      $2.50 per sq ft

983      $2.00 per sq ft

986   $2.00 per sq ft   989 $2.00 per sq ft   995 $2.75 per sq ft   997 $2.50 per sq ft   999 $1.60 per sq ft

Leaded Art Glass Colored

1000 $1.60 per sq ft

1009 $1.60 per sq ft

1012 $2.00 per sq ft

1015 $2.00 per sq ft

1018 $1.50 per sq ft   1021 $1.80 per sq ft

Leaded Art Glass Colored

1025   1026   1027   1028

Art Glass for Church Windows
Special prices on application

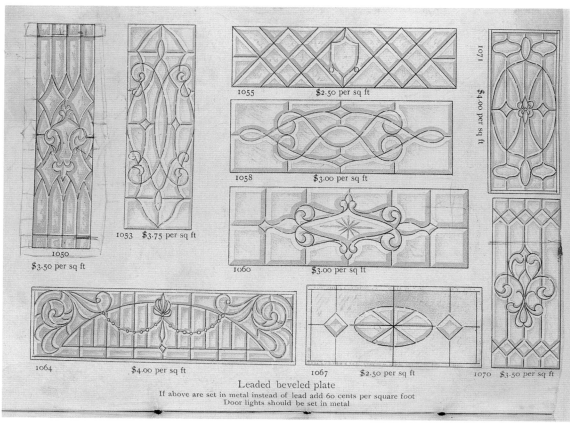

1050
$3.50 per sq ft

1053 $3.75 per sq ft

1055 $2.50 per sq ft

1058 $3.00 per sq ft

1060 $3.00 per sq ft

1071 $4.00 per sq ft

1064 $4.00 per sq ft

1067 $2.50 per sq ft

1070 $3.50 per sq ft

Leaded beveled plate
If above are set in metal instead of lead add 60 cents per square foot
Door lights should be set in metal

Mitered beveled plate
Prices furnished on application

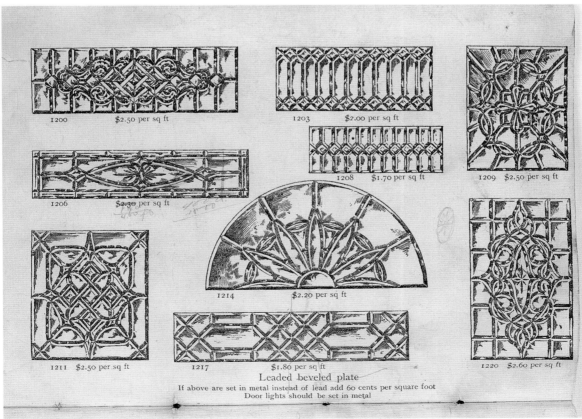

1200 $2.50 per sq ft
1203 $2.00 per sq ft
1208 $1.70 per sq ft
1209 $2.50 per sq ft
1206 $2.30 per sq ft
1214 $2.20 per sq ft
1211 $2.50 per sq ft
1217 $1.80 per sq ft
1220 $2.60 per sq ft

Leaded beveled plate
If above are set in metal instead of lead add 60 cents per square foot
Door lights should be set in metal

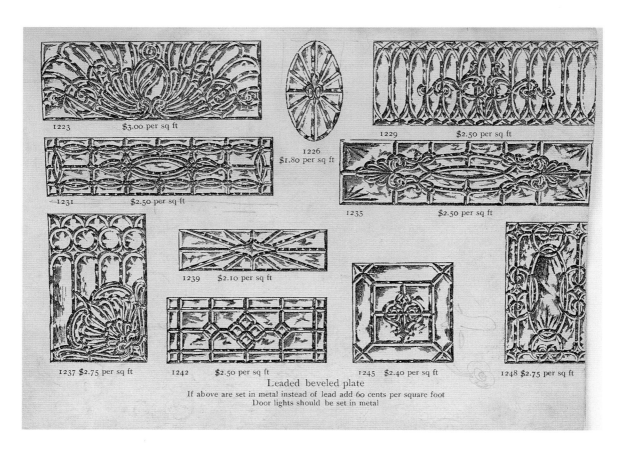

1223 $3.00 per sq ft

1226 $1.80 per sq ft

1229 $2.50 per sq ft

1231 $2.50 per sq ft

1235 $2.50 per sq ft

1239 $2.10 per sq ft

1237 $2.75 per sq ft   1242 $2.50 per sq ft   1245 $2.40 per sq ft   1248 $2.75 per sq ft

Leaded beveled plate
If above are set in metal instead of lead add 60 cents per square foot
Door lights should be set in metal

1251 $3.00 per sq ft

1254 $2.60 per sq ft

1257 $3.20 per sq ft   1260 $2.20 per sq ft   1262 $3.00 per sq ft   1265 $2.75 per sq ft

Leaded beveled plate
If above are set in metal instead of lead add 60 cents per square foot
Door lights should be set in metal

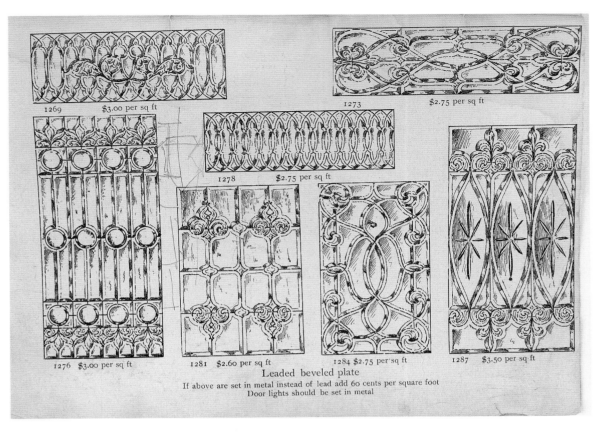

1269 $3.00 per sq ft

1273 $2.75 per sq ft

1278 $2.75 per sq ft

1276 $3.00 per sq ft   1281 $2.60 per sq ft   1284 $2.75 per sq ft   1287 $3.50 per sq ft

Leaded beveled plate

If above are set in metal instead of lead add 60 cents per square foot
Door lights should be set in metal

1302 1.90 cents per sq ft   1306 1.70 cents per sq ft   1312 1.60 cents per sq ft   1314   80 cents per sq ft

1309 1.90 cents per sq ft

1317   80 cents per sq ft   1320   90 cents per sq ft   1324   90 cents per sq ft   1327   90 cents per sq ft

1330   90 cents per sq ft   1350   60 cents per sq ft

1332   90 cents per sq ft   1336   1340   1345   1347   1352   80 cents per sq ft

1336 90 cts per sq ft   1340 70 cts per sq ft   1345 80 cts per sq ft   1347 70 cts per sq ft

Clear double strength leaded

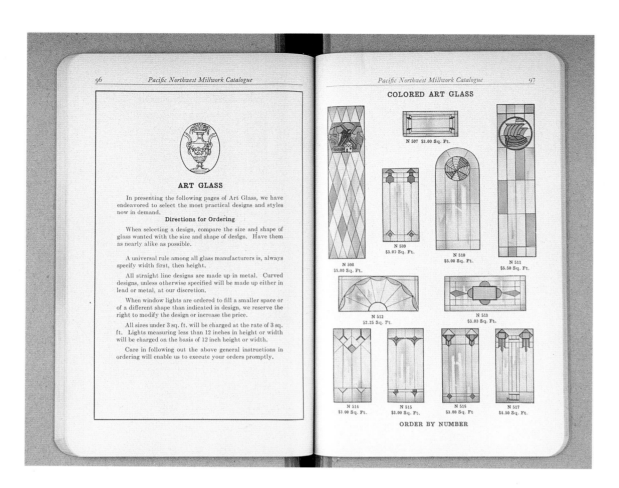

ART GLASS

In presenting the following pages of Art Glass, we have endeavored to select the most practical designs and styles now in demand.

Directions for Ordering

When selecting a design, compare the size and shape of glass wanted with the size and shape of design. Have them as nearly alike as possible.

A universal rule among all glass manufacturers is, always specify width first, then height.

All straight line designs are made up in metal. Curved designs, unless otherwise specified will be made up either in lead or metal, at our discretion.

When window lights are ordered to fill a smaller space or of a different shape than indicated in design, we reserve the right to modify the design or increase the price.

All sizes under 3 sq. ft. will be charged at the rate of 3 sq. ft. Lights measuring less than 12 inches in height or width will be charged on the basis of 12 inch height or width.

Care in following out the above general instructions in ordering will enable us to execute your orders promptly.

COLORED ART GLASS

N 507 $3.00 Sq. Ft.

N 508 $5.00 Sq. Ft.

N 509 $3.00 Sq. Ft.

N 510 $5.00 Sq. Ft.

N 511 $5.50 Sq. Ft.

N 512 $2.25 Sq. Ft.

N 513 $3.00 Sq. Ft.

N 514 $3.00 Sq. Ft.

N 515 $3.00 Sq. Ft.

N 516 $3.00 Sq. Ft.

N 517 $4.50 Sq. Ft.

ORDER BY NUMBER

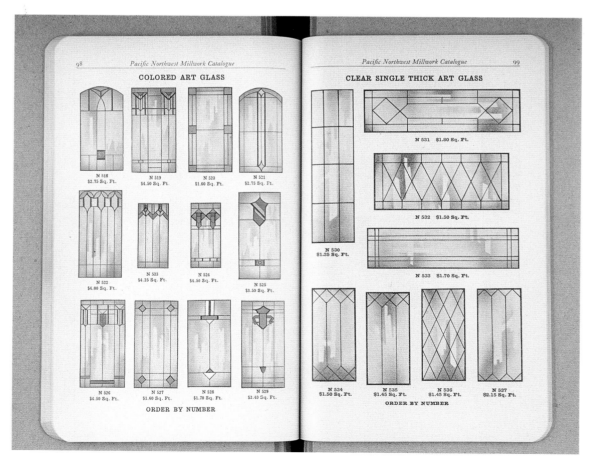

COLORED ART GLASS

CLEAR SINGLE THICK ART GLASS

N 518 $2.75 Sq. Ft.

N 519 $4.50 Sq. Ft.

N 520 $1.60 Sq. Ft.

N 521 $2.75 Sq. Ft.

N 522 $4.00 Sq. Ft.

N 523 $4.25 Sq. Ft.

N 524 $4.50 Sq. Ft.

N 525 $3.50 Sq. Ft.

N 526 $4.50 Sq. Ft.

N 527 $1.60 Sq. Ft.

N 528 $1.70 Sq. Ft.

N 529 $3.40 Sq. Ft.

ORDER BY NUMBER

N 531 $1.80 Sq. Ft.

N 532 $1.50 Sq. Ft.

N 530 $1.35 Sq. Ft.

N 533 $1.70 Sq. Ft.

N 534 $1.50 Sq. Ft.

N 535 $1.45 Sq. Ft.

N 536 $1.45 Sq. Ft.

N 537 $2.15 Sq. Ft.

ORDER BY NUMBER

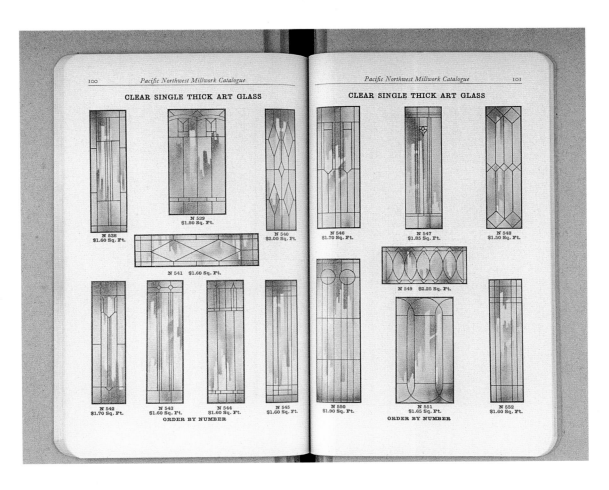

CLEAR SINGLE THICK ART GLASS

N 538
$1.60 Sq. Ft.

N 539
$1.90 Sq. Ft.

N 540
$2.00 Sq. Ft.

N 541 $1.60 Sq. Ft.

N 542
$1.70 Sq. Ft.

N 543
$1.60 Sq. Ft.

N 544
$1.60 Sq. Ft.

N 545
$1.60 Sq. Ft.

ORDER BY NUMBER

CLEAR SINGLE THICK ART GLASS

N 546
$1.70 Sq. Ft.

N 547
$1.85 Sq. Ft.

N 548
$1.50 Sq. Ft.

N 549 $2.25 Sq. Ft.

N 550
$1.90 Sq. Ft.

N 551
$1.65 Sq. Ft.

N 552
$1.60 Sq. Ft.

ORDER BY NUMBER

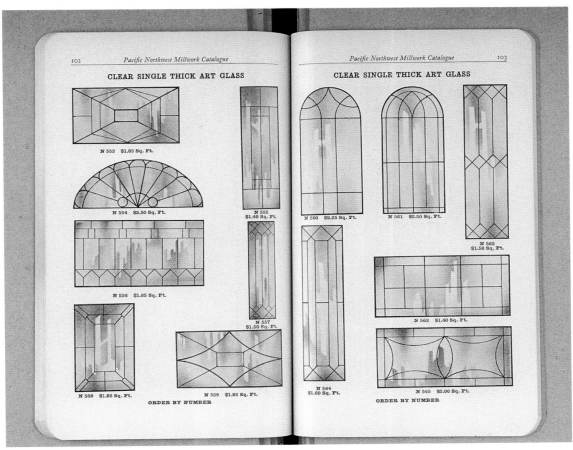

CLEAR SINGLE THICK ART GLASS

N 553 $1.85 Sq. Ft.

N 554 $2.50 Sq. Ft.

N 555
$1.40 Sq. Ft.

N 556 $1.65 Sq. Ft.

N 557
$1.50 Sq. Ft.

N 558 $1.85 Sq. Ft.

N 559 $1.85 Sq. Ft.

ORDER BY NUMBER

CLEAR SINGLE THICK ART GLASS

N 560 $2.25 Sq. Ft.

N 561 $2.50 Sq. Ft.

N 562
$1.50 Sq. Ft.

N 563 $1.40 Sq. Ft.

N 564
$1.60 Sq. Ft.

N 565 $2.00 Sq. Ft.

ORDER BY NUMBER

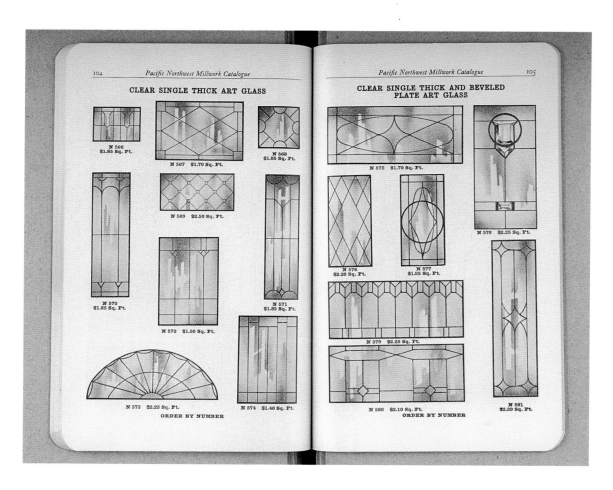

CLEAR SINGLE THICK ART GLASS

N 566
$1.85 Sq. Ft.

N 567 $1.70 Sq. Ft.

N 568
$1.85 Sq. Ft.

N 569 $2.50 Sq. Ft.

N 570
$1.85 Sq. Ft.

N 571
$1.85 Sq. Ft.

N 572 $1.50 Sq. Ft.

N 573 $2.25 Sq. Ft.

N 574 $1.40 Sq. Ft.

ORDER BY NUMBER

CLEAR SINGLE THICK AND BEVELED PLATE ART GLASS

N 575 $1.70 Sq. Ft.

N 578 $2.25 Sq. Ft.

N 576
$2.20 Sq. Ft.

N 577
$1.85 Sq. Ft.

N 579 $2.25 Sq. Ft.

N 580 $2.10 Sq. Ft.

N 581
$2.30 Sq. Ft.

ORDER BY NUMBER

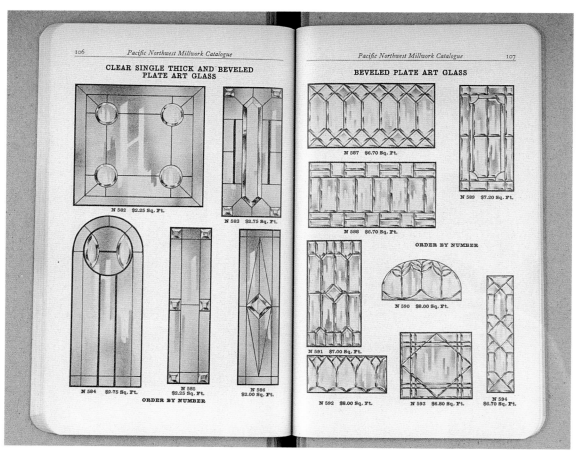

CLEAR SINGLE THICK AND BEVELED PLATE ART GLASS

N 582 $2.25 Sq. Ft.

N 583 $2.75 Sq. Ft.

N 584 $2.75 Sq. Ft.

N 585
$2.25 Sq. Ft.

N 586
$2.00 Sq. Ft.

ORDER BY NUMBER

BEVELED PLATE ART GLASS

N 587 $6.70 Sq. Ft.

N 589 $7.20 Sq. Ft.

N 588 $6.70 Sq. Ft.

ORDER BY NUMBER

N 590 $8.00 Sq. Ft.

N 591 $7.00 Sq. Ft.

N 592 $8.00 Sq. Ft.

N 593 $6.80 Sq. Ft.

N 594
$6.70 Sq. Ft.